HABANERA

A Portrait of a Cuban Family

Teresa Dovalpage

Floricanto ™

Berkeley Press is an imprint of Inter American Development, Inc.

Floricanto[M] Press

650 Castro Street, 120-331

Mountain View, California 94041

(415) 552-1879

www. floricantopress. com

ISBN: 978-1-888205-37-4

"Por nuestra cultura hablarán nuestros libros. Our books shall speak for our culture. "

Roberto Cabello-Argandoña,

Editor

HABANERA

A Portrait of a Cuban Family

First Part

San Anastasio Street: Cooking in Minutes

Chapter 1

The Havana cemetery was my first playground. Ponciano Querejeta, my maternal grandfather, liked to stroll by the graves and to read under the palm trees. He often sat on a bench and sang in his baritone voice. His favorite tune came from the Spanish *zarzuela Los Gavilanes*: "*Oh, mi aldea...cuánto el alma se recrea al volverte a contemplar*." (Oh, my village... my soul cheers up when I see you again.) No wonder the few people we met looked at him funny.

The cemetery smelled of grass, rotten leaves and damp earth. Our usual companions were an elderly guy named Amenodoro, a clandestine flower vendor and some mourners in black. "*Hola*, Ponciano," Amenodoro always said when we passed by. "Have a good time."

My grandfather had showed me our family's tomb, where a sad-looking angel spread its marble wings over the deceased Querejetas. "This mausoleum looks just like one in the Père-Lachaise," Ponciano said. He had lived in Paris during his youth and was a hardcore Francophile. "It's worth several thousand pesos. Someday I'll be buried here. And so will you, Dolorcitas."

"That's cool," I answered, not really sure of what

"buried" meant.

The only thing I didn't like was to be called Dolorcitas when my name was Longina. But I had already learned that my grandfather, a cranky, tall and lean old man, didn't act the way other people did. I didn't mind it, though. At that time I was closer to him than to anybody else. And I thought of the cemetery as the most fun-filled place in Havana, even better than the Guanabo beach and Lenin Park.

My father, Papucho, said that I had no business running around a graveyard. "Why don't you take Longina to an amusement park instead?" he asked Ponciano.

"I'd rather spend time on sacred soil," my grandfather replied.

"What's sacred about decomposing bodies?"

My grandma scolded Papucho, "Hey, show more respect to the dead!"

"Respect? That graveyard strolling is sickening."

But Papucho was the last monkey in the family zoo. He had neither voice nor vote. Ponciano ignored him and our visits to the cemetery continued.

We would sit near a grave covered with fresh flowers, candles and bananas tied with blue ribbons. The tomb belonged to Amelia *La Milagrosa* and her family. My grandfather knew the story of its fleshless tenants and cheerfully shared it with me.

Amelia, a young woman who had died during childbirth in 1901, was buried with her stillborn son at her feet. Five years later their bodies were found intact, the baby nestled in his mother's arms. Journalists wrote about them in *El Mundo* and *La Marina*, the most important Cuban newspapers before the revolution. Soon stories sprouted like the grass around their grave. Amelia's influence had saved a child from typhus. She had healed a paralyzed girl. Her devotees called her The Miracle

Woman and a priest spoke of canonizing her.

Ponciano didn't believe in miracles but was convinced that mother and child, or at least Amelia, had been buried alive. The topic intrigued me. What happened when people were buried alive? Was it...uncomfortable? Were they ever rescued? "I will tell you someday," he promised. "Edgar Allan Poe wrote a few stories about that."

I invented a game called funeral party. Pretending that our backyard was the cemetery, I would take a doll to her grave while the other dolls followed and chanted, *Oh, mi aldea...cuánto el alma se recrea al volverte a contemplar*. My grandma frowned when she saw me engrossed in it. She shook her head and called me a quirky girl, but didn't intervene until the night I woke up crying because *La Milagrosa* had come for me.

I was quirky, no doubt. While some kids have imaginary friends, I had an imaginary enemy. She was two years older than I, pug-nosed and red-haired. She didn't have a name. I called her *la otra*, the other girl. Actually, *la otra* wasn't an enemy as much as someone to argue with. My best friends in real life were Carlitos and Sandra, the next-door kids. But Carlitos and I didn't fight because he was my "boyfriend," which meant we always did what *he* wanted. Sandra was a year younger and such a sweet-tempered child that it was difficult to argue with her. She also had a strong sense of communal property.

"Here is your doll," she would say, offering me one of her made-in-the-USSR Aniuskas or Shashenkas.

"No, Sandra, it's yours," I answered.

"What's the difference?"

The three of us played, ate and even napped together when we had the opportunity. However, Carlitos and Sandra were not *family*. "Why do you have to run after these people like a Chihuahua dog after a bone?" my grandma scolded me when I spent more than two hours at our neighbors' house. "Leave them alone and don't be such a pest."

I often missed having a brother or a sister. But being an only child had advantages. I was spoiled rotten. When I asked for her make-up kit, my grandma let me paint my lips, eyelashes and cheeks until I looked like a clown. As for Ponciano, even if he had seen me molding figures with my own *caca,* he wouldn't have said a word. (He might have even helped me.)

My parents lived in a distant world of their own. They came home around six o'clock. I went to bed at eight. I didn't even know what they did outside the house. On weekends they became Papucho and Ma mère—it was Ponciano's idea that I call my mother Ma mère—and fussed over me. Used to being around my grandparents, I saw Papucho and Ma mère as kind strangers that took me to the Alameda Movie Theater and to Las Ruinas restaurant in Lenin Park, but I wasn't sure they were *family,* either. I thought that all mothers were supposed to be like Sandra's, who stayed home cooking for her kids, had long, shiny hair and wore flowery muumuus.

The adults argued among themselves. My grandmother called Papucho a lazy, good-for-nothing *cabrón,* while Ma mère tended to defend him. But they all fawned over me. Having no reason to fight with anybody, *la otra* became the recipient of all the insults I learned. The fact that I didn't know what they meant didn't stop me from using them.

"You are a bad girl, a whore!" I told her once.

My grandma didn't pay attention to our imaginary arguments. But that day Ma mère was around. After asking, with a horrified expression, what I had meant by that, she forbade me to talk to *la otra* again. Of course,

I didn't obey her.

§ § §

One afternoon my grandfather took a leather-bound copy of Poe's *Complete Works* and read "The Premature Burial" by Amelia's grave. Frightened but thrilled, I asked for more. He went on with "The Cask of Amontillado." Before leaving he recited "The Raven." "Bravo, Ponciano!" Amenodoro yelled, shattering the heavy silence that draped the cemetery like a shroud.

Ponciano bowed.

That night *La Milagrosa* came to me in a dream. She was a pale, green-eyed woman who pressed a pillow against my face while singing, *Oh, mi aldea...cuánto el alma se recrea al volverte a contemplar.* I screamed, vomited and refused to go back to sleep.

I knew better than to mention our Poe readings, or, God forbid, Amelia's story, but Ma mère suspected that the walks in the cemetery had caused my nervous breakdown. She ordered Ponciano to stay away from me. This time, my grandma agreed. "You can't even take Longina to the grocery store," they told him. "Or we all will move out of the house!"

That was Ponciano's biggest fear. Not to be left alone, since I suspect that he would have been happier living on his own, but having to divide the family home—the only way any of us could move out. Despite my pleas he didn't take me again to the cemetery. "You can't keep your mouth shut," he grunted when I begged to let me go with him. "Get lost!"

A few weeks later my grandma bought a Chinese dollhouse on the black market and gave it to me on condition that I would stop playing funeral party.

Oh, mi aldea...cuánto el alma se recrea al volverte a contemplar.

§ § §

Maybe it wasn't a bad idea to keep Ponciano away from me. He sauntered through life shrouded in a mysterious illness known as neurasthenia. He had inherited it from his mother, Doña Lola Fontán, whose name my grandma always pronounced with pursed lips.

My great-grandmother had been a neurotic, according to my grandma. "An eccentric," Ponciano rectified. He spoke of her with reverence and called her Mama Lola. Doña Lola had attended the musical academy Pro-Arte and could have been a professional opera singer, Ponciano boasted. She sang Spanish *zarzuelas* in the buff, my grandma said, and had as much rhythm as a cracked bidet. A faithful reader of *Orígenes* magazine, Doña Lola had also written a book of poetry. But the language was so convoluted that few people understood it. The book was never published.

I overheard the Doña Lola stories when the adults talked among themselves because they avoided mentioning her when I was around. "She died before your birth," my grandma told me once, reluctantly. "Ponciano wanted to name you after her, but I didn't allow it. What if you turned out to be as...eccentric as she was? You are already goofy enough without anyone's help."

My name came from Manuel Corona's most famous ballad, *Longina*. But Ponciano never use it to address me. When we were by ourselves, he called me Dolorcitas, which was quite confusing at first.

My grandma loved ballads. Her Crosley record player was always on. *Septeto Habanero* and *danzón* king Barbarito Diez fought the voices of foreign news reporters that came from Ponciano's room. My grandma, who couldn't stand the political talk, would bark, "Ponciano, *viejo*, turn that crap off, will you?"

My grandfather's response was turning it up full blast while laughing quietly under his breath. He had a peculiar, sardonic, scary *he-he-he*. "Just like his mother," my grandma would mutter, "She could spend *hours* listening to the same cracked record."

By the time I was five years old, Doña Lola had attained the proportions of a mythical figure in my imagination. I wouldn't stop asking about her. What did she look like? Was she tall or short? Could I see a picture of her? All these questions annoyed my grandma to no end. "Don't be so snoopy, *niña*," she warned me. "Her spirit is still around and it may come after you."

I wished she had kept that comment to herself. I would recall it the day Doña Lola approached me in the middle of a hurricane, demanding her lost book.

"But was she beautiful?" I insisted.

"She used to be a very attractive woman," my grandma admitted. "*Très chic*, as Ponciano said. But because of the neurasthenia, she looked like a witch in her last years. She wouldn't even wash herself. *I* had to bathe her. Uff!"

I later discovered that a faded portrait that hung in my grandfather's bedroom was Doña Lola's—a black-haired, green-eyed, long-nosed lady with a big mole on her right cheek. I found her image vaguely familiar but couldn't remember where I had seen it before.

Ponciano had inherited his mother's aquiline nose and green eyes, as well as many of her quirks. He disliked bathrooms and didn't bathe often, but always wore old dark suits and matching ties. And he spent hours locked up in a bedroom that smelled of dirt, urine and stale bread. There he ate, read, slept and listened to Radio

France International and the Voice of America on an asthmatic Motorola. He placed empty glass bottles behind the door to make sure that no one would enter when he was asleep.

Despite the stench, I liked to peek in. Once I managed to enter and saw Doña Lola's portrait, an unmade bed, an armoire, several cardboard boxes and a porcelain urinal. That urinal, which Ponciano had bought in Paris fifty years before, was the center of a malodorous routine. While the rest of the family ate, my grandfather would pass by to empty the urinal in a bathroom adjacent to the dining room. Switching dinner times didn't work. He watched us closely and every night when we were having soup he strutted by, wrapped in a halo of pee and *he-he-he*ing.

I was getting ready to open the armoire when my grandma caught me.

"Get out of here!" she yelled, dragging me back to the hall. "You have the rest of the house to play in. Stay away from this room!"

With my ties to Ponciano so suddenly severed, I became more attached to my grandmother. She had a generous heart, a colossal ass and curves to match. She loved everybody, particularly younger guys, and made no secret of it. Some people said she was a tease. She had a way of crossing her legs that Ma mère had forbidden me to imitate.

Ponciano resented any man, no matter how young or how old, that visited our house. He had probably called my grandma the questionable word "whore" during one of their frequent fights. My grandparents occupied separate rooms. My grandma slept in mine and Ponciano in the master bedroom. But she still cooked for him, as she did for all of us, and sometimes washed his clothes.

Habanera

My grandma's name was Eugenia but everybody called her Muñeca (Doll) because of her good looks. When she was in her early fifties, she didn't seem one day over forty. She kept her brown hair waist-long and was the proud owner of a mountain-like ass, *un culo piramidal*, which she wiggled conceitedly.

She never took me to the neighborhood park where the other grandmothers got together to gossip, knit and exchange recipes. Muñeca refused to be around old people. "Wrinkles are contagious," she claimed. She also hated the boys in roller skates that came dangerously close to her high-heeled shoes. She preferred to go to Coppelia, Havana's most renowned ice cream parlor. It was in El Vedado and we needed to take several buses to get there. But Muñeca didn't mind the trip. In Coppelia she met a guy named Ramoncito and they laughed and held hands while we waited in line. Ramoncito was bald, in his forties, and constantly complained about *la vieja*, a nagging woman who was, no doubt, his wife.

After having a sundae or a banana split, the three of us walked to Antonio Maceo Park. My grandma and Ramoncito sent me to play with other children and they retreated to a bench sheltered by overgrown bushes.

"Run, jump, find someone to play with," Muñeca said. "You need to get some fresh air! And don't come back until I call you. *Anda*!"

I tried to obey her but ended up playing alone most of the times since I was too shy to approach other kids. And yet, that was more interesting that staying home. Though I was barely five years old, I realized that some illicit hanky-panky was going on there. But it never bothered me. On the contrary, being a witness to my grandma's affair made me feel special, smart and secretly powerful. The only thing I didn't like about Antonio Maceo Park was the presence of carrion birds, *las auras tiñosas* that circled overhead because there was a garbage dump nearby. They had featherless red heads and yellowish feet and didn't seem afraid of people. I hid among the bushes when they began to fly too low.

Muñeca had established two strict rules about our Coppelia outings. I wasn't supposed to call her "grandma" in front of Ramoncito, but "aunt." "I am *Tía* Eugenia, remember. Or just Muñeca. Don't embarrass me." And I was to keep mum about Ramoncito. "Don't ever mention him to your mother or to Ponciano, hear?" she warned me.

It was a family habit to add the word "hear?" at the end of sentences when important matters were discussed.

"I know that!" I replied, offended. Despite Ponciano's opinion, I didn't consider myself a snitch.

The furtive visits to Coppelia went on for years. I ate chocolate, vanilla and mango ice cream coated with the piquant sauce of forbidden love. When Ma mère asked where we had been for so long, my grandma always had a good excuse ready. The most common one was that she had taken me to a gathering sponsored by *Los Pioneritos* (The Little Pioneers) where they taught kids to march and to sing revolutionary songs.

§ § §

The first time I heard a revolutionary song was not at a *Los Pioneritos* meeting (which I never attended, by the way) but a Saturday morning, at home, while a voluntary work session took place outside. A crew of women led by Ofelia, the president of our neighborhood Committee for the Defense of the Revolution, was sweeping the street. With their red kerchiefs and black berets, à la Che Guevara, they looked like giant ladybugs. They sang *La*

Internacional at the top of their lungs,

Arise ye workers from your slumbers
Arise ye prisoners of want
For reason in revolt now thunders
And at last ends the age of cant.

People called the volunteers *comecandelas*—fire-eaters. The title was reserved for earnest revolutionaries. *Comecandelas* were more Marxist than Marx and more communist than Fidel's underwear.

Barbarita, the Vigilance commissary, was a *comecandela*. She wore tight pants that drew attention to her monumental *culón*, almost as big as my grandmother's. Active in all the voluntary work sessions, she also organized Red Sundays, when people went to their jobs as usual but donated their salary to the government.

"Come on, comrades!" she shouted to her crew. "Move those brooms! We can't let *El Comandante* down!"

The morning of the voluntary work *Celia Cruz* had knocked at our door at seven-thirty A.M. Our neighbor's real name was Juana Díaz, but she bore a striking resemblance to the queen of salsa. *Celia Cruz* was a clandestine *colera* who would stand in line, holding a place for others, in exchange for ten or twenty pesos, depending on how long the line was. She was also the first one to know what had arrived at the grocery store and the butcher's. My grandfather was a *colero* too, though he specialized in high-end restaurants.

"Guess what came to the hardware store for the C-34 coupon," *Celia Cruz* told my grandma, gasping. "Alarm clocks!"

Muñeca shrugged, buttoning her checkered dressing gown. "So what, *chica*?" she replied with a yawn. "Let us sleep!"

Celia Cruz left, open-mouthed and offended. She

was used to being thanked profusely when she brought such good news.

Everything, from food to clothes, from vacation trips to travel permits, was given to people or "came" to them. Beans, sugar, coffee and toilet paper "came" to the grocery store, and bread to *la panadería*. Four yards of polyester fabric per person "came" twice a year to the clothing store where they could be bought with the A-33 coupon. The A-34 coupon gave women the right to buy a brassiere. Too bad it was the same that corresponded to a pair of panties.

Make-up was so scarce that when it "came" to the local store the lines were three blocks long. Electric fans, radios and TV sets were assigned to workers according to their revolutionary standing. The fact that alarm clocks had "come" to the hardware store was, in fact, remarkable. In normal times Muñeca would have shown more appreciation to our neighbor. But those weren't normal times.

The day *Celia Cruz* was so disdainfully dismissed my parents and grandmother were flying high on the precarious wings of hope. They were planning to run away from ration cards and waiting lines, from the calls to do voluntary work and the vigilant eyes of the *comecandelas*. They had requested an official permit to travel to *La Yuma,* as people called the United States.

Going to *La Yuma* had been a bone of contention in my family for years. In the early sixties, when Cecilia, my grandmother's older sister, went to Miami, Muñeca wanted to join her. Ponciano opposed this proposal, saying that Fidel Castro wouldn't last more than a few months in power. Later on, the migratory agreements between Cuba and the United States came to an end and direct flights Havana-Miami were cancelled. When the Mariel boatlift took place in 1980, Ponciano, grudgingly, agreed to leave with the whole family. I was a baby then. But the motorboat that Cecilia and her husband sent to pick us up wasn't allowed to enter the Mariel port. It sailed under the Dominican Republic flag and only American boats were authorized to take Cubans to the United States.

This time around things would be different, Muñeca hoped. Upon hearing that the government was letting people go again, she dispatched Papucho to get our emigration forms. Her sister Cecilia had already agreed to send us the plane tickets, which had to be paid for in American dollars.

Prospective emigrants needed to fill out a form asking for permission to leave the country. The forms were extremely hard to find. So as to get them, people waited in line for days in front of the emigration department offices where they were harassed and called *gusanos*, worms, and unpatriotic bastards by the *comecandelas*.

Ma mère and my grandparents lived in a state of permanent frenzy while Papucho waited in line. Words I had never heard popped up in conversations that often degenerated into fights. Some had a disturbing resonance, like *la renuncia*, the official giving up of all our possessions, including the house that had been in the family for generations. *La renuncia*! Ponciano pronounced it as if it burned his mouth. But Muñeca was in seventh heaven. She was a fervent *gusana*, and proud of it. "At last, we are going to leave this God-forsaken country!" she said. "Soon we will be in the North!"

Older people said the North, *el Norte*. Younger generations, like my parents', preferred *La Yuma*.

"But if we leave, I'll lose everything," my grandfather croaked. "This house, all the money in the bank, the furniture—"

"*No jodas*, Ponciano Querejeta!" Muñeca replied, exasperated. *No jodas*, cut the crap, was one of her favorite phrases. "*What* haven't you lost already? The house isn't ours anymore. We aren't even allowed to sell or rent it. Pesos are worthless. The furniture is junk."

I surveyed our living room. The leather sofa and the marble-top coffee table didn't look like junk to me. Ponciano voiced the same opinion.

"It doesn't matter," Muñeca shrugged. "It's only stuff. We can buy more. We'll start over again in Miami."

"I'm too old to start over again and I don't like Miami. If we were going to Paris, I would consider it."

"Ponciano, we have no one in Paris!"

"And I want to be buried in the Havana cemetery. Our mausoleum is worth. . . "

"Forget the mausoleum! You aren't dead yet!"

"And tell me, who is going to take care...?" he started to say.

Muñeca cut him off, "We *all* will leave. No one is going to be left behind. Shut up now," and she pointed at me.

"But who is going to support us?" Ponciano insisted. "I can't work anymore, you are just a housewife and Carmen doesn't speak English. Ah, and if you are counting on your son-in-law, we'll starve to death, hear?"

"He's your son-in-law too! And he can...he can *change*," Muñeca said, though she didn't sound convinced. "He has potential."

Ponciano smirked. "*Merde*." Unlike Muñeca, my grandfather didn't swear a lot. And when he did, he favored French.

"You are nothing but a crepehanger," she shot at him.

"I have my feet firmly planted on the ground while yours are in the clouds. I am not going anywhere but you can do as you please. *Au revoir*!"

Habanera

I was trying to make sense of all that when Muñeca turned to me.

"Go play with your dollhouse," she said. "*Anda*!"

Her "*anda*!" (go!) reminded me of the meetings with Ramoncito, when she sent me to get some fresh air. She was up to something. I left the living room, but tiptoed back and hid behind the door.

"We won't get the exit permits, anyway," Ponciano was saying. "And the whole family will be buried in the Havana cemetery."

"Stop giving us *mal agüero*!"

Mal agüero is the harming power of words. My grandfather, people said, was an expert in channeling bad luck.

"You will see, old woman."

"Shut up!"

Muñeca stormed out as Ponciano *he-he-he*ed. I went back to my room, struggling to understand what all the fuss was about. Exit permits, *la renuncia*, visas, *au revoir*...The new words flew inside my head, scary and menacing—like carrion birds.

Chapter 2

We lived in a quiet suburb called Lawton. Every evening Muñeca and I sat on the front porch when the first fireflies appeared and the flowers of the night-blooming jasmine opened their petals. Their scent mixed with the smell of the rosemary, basil and cilantro plants that grew in the backyard. My grandma rocked back and forth and sang old songs of love. Her favorite was *Se fue* by Ernesto Lecuona,

Se fue para no volver,
Se fue sin decirme adiós.
Muy lejos de mí se fue
Matando mi ensueño de amor.
(He left, never to return,
He left, without saying goodbye.
He left, faraway from me,
Killing my dream of love.)

Would we also have to leave, never to return?

I had finally understood what *la renuncia* and the emigration forms were all about, and I didn't like it. The idea of leaving Cuba and our old, but ample and fresh house, frightened me. I had just started school and teachers told us every day that we lived in the best country in the whole world, a lucky island where the government guaranteed freedom, health and education to everyone.

La Yuma, on the other hand, was an evil empire full of criminals who killed each other in their crowded streets. In Miami people were crammed into tiny apartments, worked ten hours a day and never saw a ray of sum. "Americans are racist," said *Maestra* Mercedes, my first grade teacher. "They hate Latinos and do not allow them to eat in the same restaurants as Gringos. The Cubans who go to *La Yuma* become second-class citizens."

"Why can't we just stay?" I asked Muñeca after she and Ponciano had discussed the issue for the umpteenth time.

"Because I'm tired of living under Castro's thumb," she answered.

Every morning at school we repeated, "*Comandante en Jefe, ordene*!" and sang revolutionary hymns that praised Fidel and his comrades.

"But he's our leader, grandma. Isn't he—like—the best?"

"Of course not! He is a dictator! He keeps an eye on everybody, knows even what one whispers in private and has taken over the country."

"Our house too? And the mausoleum?"

"Don't ask so many questions, *niña*. Politics isn't for kids. And don't mind what your teachers say. We are going to Miami, hear?"

I got so panicky about the intended trip that I vomited on the spot. *Gua*! Forgetting her *La Yuma* dreams, Muñeca gave me a glass of water and hurried to prepare chamomile tea.

The acid taste of vomit was as familiar to me as my own skinny self. Because of my "nervous stomach," as my grandma called it, I constantly threw up after meals. Sometimes I was able to hold it if I went to bed and lay down for ten minutes. But most days I didn't even have time to leave the dining room and *gua*ed there. No wonder I didn't like to eat. What for, if everything was going to come back up in the end?

My lack of appetite was a source of mortification for everybody in the family, particularly Muñeca. She took it as a personal insult because she was the cook, and considered herself a good one. One evening at dinnertime she looked at my untouched dish and shook her head.

"If you don't make an effort to eat, you are going to die," she said. "You'll get thinner and thinner until you turn into a spirit. Just like that, paf! And then...no more Longina!"

"Do spirits need to eat?" I asked, tongue-in-cheek.

"No. They can't eat, play with their buddies or watch television."

"I want to be a spirit, then. Like Doña Lola."

"I've asked you not to talk about her."

"*Gua*!"

"*Ay*, not again! Why are you puking when you haven't even had a bite yet?"

My grandma ended up eating all the *papitas fritas* she had cooked for me, soaked in mayonnaise. I couldn't stand those French fries. Even their smell made me feel nauseated.

Other times she made somber remarks about my future, "You'll never be 'developed,' I'm afraid." ("To develop," in Muñeca's vocabulary, was to blossom into a young woman.) You won't be able to find a boyfriend and you'll become a spinster, lonely and sour."

"Developed" women like herself had big breasts and well-cushioned asses. Ma mère, however, was slender and had a modest butt. I took comfort in the fact that she had married Papucho, a handsome man, despite her obvious "underdevelopment." There was still hope for me.

Doctors couldn't find anything wrong with me. They concluded that the vomiting fits were caused by anxiety. Now, the idea of leaving Cuba for a place where we were not welcome made my stomach more nervous than ever before.

§ § §

Papucho stayed in line for three days in front of the emigration building, waiting to get the forms. Despite her initial enthusiasm, Muñeca began to lose hope. "That good-for-nothing drunk will come back empty-handed," she said to Ma mère. "I should have gone myself."

It was the first time that Papucho's alcoholism was mentioned around me. I had noticed that he often acted funny. He confused or slurred words, forgot to turn off the oven, walked unsteadily. . . Some mornings he got up late, said he had a headache and didn't go to work. I knew that Muñeca and Ponciano didn't like him too well. But did that mean that he was *un borracho*, a drunk?

My invisible companion and I discussed the "good-for-nothing drunk" comment at length. I said it was one of Muñeca's exaggerated claims. But *la otra* maintained that my grandma was right. "We'll starve to death in *La Yuma* if we depend only on Papucho," she said.

"You are just like Ponciano," I answered. "A crepe-hanger!"

At last Papucho came home, grinning proudly. He was *not* empty-handed. His white teeth sparkled when he handed my grandma the emigration forms. "We have one foot in Miami now!"

Muñeca kissed him. "But you have to stop drinking when we get to *el Norte*," she warned him. "Ponciano is getting old so you'll become the man of the house."

"No problem," my father answered with a reassuring smile. "I'll take care of the family. Stonemasons make a lot of money in *La Yuma*. And I'll stop drinking today. I won't touch another drop of alcohol, I swear."

They hugged each other.

"I'm sorry I've given you such a hard time all these

years, Papucho," Muñeca sniffled. "You are a good man."

"Not really. I haven't been a jewel, you know? But it's time for me to shape up. And I will."

Ma mère joined the embrace, also crying. It was a highly emotional scene that Ponciano watched, with a malevolent grin, from his urine-smelling room.

§ § §

In the forties and fifties Cubans only needed a tourist visa to travel to *La Yuma*. Before the revolution, Muñeca had visited Miami a few times to shop and party. She had learned to dance the jitterbug in a beach club called the Colony House, which she remembered fondly. "I met a Manhattan banker there and he was crazy for me," she confessed with a sly smile. "The guy had more money than God. If I had married him, I'd be living like a princess now."

"Was he handsome?" I asked her.

"Not bad looking at all. Tall, blond, blue-eyed...But he didn't have much *sandunga*."

"What's *sandunga*?"

"Sex appeal, *niña*," she swayed her hips suggestively.

"What did Ponciano say about the banker?"

"He didn't know. Such a bore, he never traveled with me...After his father died he got so attached to Doña Lola that he wouldn't leave her alone, even for a weekend. But that didn't stop me from having a good time."

I had heard that my grandma was *la candela*, pretty hot, and I began to realize why.

"Good times can come back," she went on. "Pray every night to *Papa Dios* and ask him to let us go to *el Norte*. Children's prayers are always heard."

"Who is *Papa Dios*?" I asked.

"God almighty. He watches you all the time. He's everywhere and he knows everything."

"Is he *El Comandante*?"

"Don't say blasphemies! I should teach you the catechism or you'll end up an atheist, a communist or something worse."

In Muñeca's old photos Miami didn't look like an evil land. It was a blurred kingdom of martini glasses, beach hats and sleepy-eyed dancers.

"And there is good food in *La Yuma*," my grandma said, smacking her lips. "Olives, apples, Brie cheese, steaks . . . all yummy stuff. No ration cards, no waiting lines . . . Supermarkets are full of everything you can think of. Haven't you heard a verse that says,

Si quieres comer jamón y saborear mantequilla,

Tírate al Malecón y nada noventa millas?"

(If you want to eat ham and taste butter,

Jump in the Malecón waters and swim ninety miles.)

I didn't care much for ham or *mantequilla* and didn't know what supermarkets were. There was only one grocery store in the neighborhood, with empty shelves and a lonely, cantankerous clerk. We were not allowed to buy food anywhere else.

Besides, I liked Lawton and the peaceful evenings we spent on the front porch. And I was in love with Carlitos, who kissed me under the jasmine tree that grew between our backyards and had promised to marry me. But if Muñeca left I couldn't stay, could I? I couldn't say *au revoir* to her!

La otra and I had long and heated arguments. I rooted for moving to *La Yuma*, at least temporarily. She preferred to stay. "I won't follow you to Miami," she threatened me.

I shrugged, pretending that I didn't care. I did, though. What was I going to do without her, without Carlitos, without Sandra? And the mausoleum! Who was going to occupy my place in that beautiful marble grave?

A few days after the emigration forms were filled out and sent, the Ministry of the Interior notified the local Committee for the Defense of the Revolution that our family had applied to leave the country. Barbarita called my father "an ungrateful worm, for whom the revolution was made," alluding to his humble origins. (He was the son of a Galician maid and of a stevedore.) As for my mother and maternal grandparents, *los* Querejeta, they were "despicable members of the defeated bourgeoisie."

But Barbarita had a soft spot for me. One day she came by when I was playing on the front porch. "You guys should stay, Longina," she said. "Life is hard now because of the Yankee blockade, but we will win the battle under *El Comandante*'s guidance. And Cuba is your homeland."

"Homeland" was too abstract a concept. Did it mean the jasmine tree or chocolate ice cream in Coppelia?

"Here is a photo of *El Comandante*," Barbarita handed me a wallet calendar with the portrait of a bearded man in green fatigues. Then she told me about *la Campaña de Alfabetización*. During the 1961 Literacy Campaign, thousands of peasants had been taught to read and write by volunteer teachers. They all wrote letters to *El Comandante* expressing their gratitude and praising him. "I was a volunteer teacher myself," said Barbarita. "Remember: every good thing that happens in this country is a gift from Fidel."

She left singing a popular *comecandela* song, "*Cuba,*

qué linda es Cuba. Quien la defiende la quiere más." (Cuba, how pretty is Cuba. Those who defend it love it the best.)

I hid the calendar inside Aniuska, a Soviet doll whose head was easily separated from her body. The image of *El Comandante* and my concept of *Papa Dios* blended together, resulting in an almighty, bearded sovereign who read all the letters his subjects sent to him.

The following day I wrote the first of many messages to that powerful being.

Dear *Comandante*,

My parents and Muñeca want to go to Miami but Ponciano and *la otra* don't. I am not sure if I want to go or not. Could you give me a hint?

Gracias.

Longina

I hadn't heard of the Post Office yet. My letter joined the calendar inside Aniuska's plastic belly.

To cover all the bases, Muñeca asked a *santera* for help. Though she called herself a Catholic, my grandma also believed in the Afro-Cuban gods, the *orishas*. Her friend Caridad, a Santería priestess, came in with a cigar, a bottle of Florida water and a bag full of a mysterious brown powder that smelled like chicken *caca*.

Caridad sprinkled the four corners of every room in the house with Florida water. She trotted from the front porch to the kitchen puffing on her cigar and blew the content of the bag on all of us, except Ponciano, who refused to participate in the ceremony. Muñeca made a promise to *San Lázaro*. She would walk from *Los Pasionistas* church, in Lawton, to *San Lázaro*'s sanctuary in the faraway town of Santiago de las Vegas, if the permit was granted. My mother and Papucho offered to accompany her on her pilgrimage.

But would *El Comandante* let us go to *La Yuma*?

"Never!" *la otra* declared. "We will *all* be buried in our old mausoleum. Mark my words."

Ponciano had said exactly the same thing.

Every morning Muñeca watched for the mailman, waiting for the emigration department's response. Every afternoon she took out her old photo albums and babbled about the Colony House, martinis and cocktails, and her wealthy friends in Miami Beach. Every night Ponciano swore he would never leave Cuba, where he had obligations to fulfill, and my grandma insulted him. We had applied as a *núcleo familiar*, a complete family. If one refused to go, the others would have to start the process all over again and were likely to be turned down. The main reason the government had for letting people go was to take over their houses and assign them to revolutionary families, and this couldn't be done if somebody was left behind.

Instead of *Se fue*, Muñeca now sang *I Left my Heart in San Francisco* to practice her English. My grandfather responded by bellowing *La Marseillaise*. *My way* clashed with *La Vie en Rose*. Their musical skirmishes lasted hours. At first they were comical but became boring and nerve-wrecking after several weeks. I used to cover my head with a pillow when the inharmonious recital started.

Papucho kept his word. He didn't get drunk again after bringing home the emigration forms and he didn't miss work anymore. But he had also gotten cranky. He even yelled at Ma mère, which was unusual for him. She responded by swearing at him with words borrowed from Muñeca. I felt as if I was walking in a mine field as those described in the book *Heroic Vietnam* that we read at school. My grandma would send me to play with Carlitos and Sandra when the tempers soared.

Days crawled, filled with high expectations and constant fights. And then, to soothe the tensions, Muñeca decided to celebrate, for the first time in years, a Christmas party at home.

Chapter 3

It was a party doomed from the start, when the cracks that would finally erode the family began to appear. But at that time no one knew it. And we whispered to each other *Feliz Navidad*, a phrase that had the alluring jingle of prohibited words.

"Merry Christmas" was a taboo greeting that only the *gusanos* used. In the official calendar *Navidad* was an ordinary day. If it fell during the week, people went to their jobs as usual. When it fell on a weekend, they were asked to do voluntary work. Decorating the house with Christmas ornaments was also a bourgeois trend. So was singing *Silent Night* and *Little Drummer Boy*. Those who kept pre-*Comandante* plastic trees hid them in bedrooms or kitchens, afraid of the informers that peeked in when one least expected it. Only in churches were Christmas trees displayed, from December to January. *Nuestra Señora del Carmen*, in Infanta Avenue, exhibited an elaborately ornamented *árbol de Navidad* and a larger-than-life Nativity scene. *Los Pasionistas*, in Lawton, had a more modest set.

Our next-door neighbors, Tony and Silvana, were the only ones in San Anastasio Street who hung a string of Christmas lights in their living room. It glowed faintly and several bulbs were burned out, but the *comecandelas* noticed and asked the offenders to remove it. They refused. Adding insult to injury, Rita, Silvana's sister, sat on the front porch to knit sweaters with Christmas motifs for Carlitos and Sandra. Tony, a wiry schoolteacher, played *Silent Night* on his violin. Silvana took the kids to *Los Pasionistas* Church for Midnight Mass.

Habanera

My folks never went to church, but celebrated *Navidad* at home with Cuba's traditional Christmas dinner: roasted pork served with white rice, black beans and *yuca* with a garlic sauce. *Yuca*, rice and beans were sold in Havana, but pigs were black market items and had to come straight from the countryside.

We went in together with another family on one. Every December, Papucho and his buddy Gerardo took the Pinar del Río train and traveled to Piloto, a small town, to buy a Christmas pig. Gerardo's cousin, the *guajiro* Miguel, sold a few animals clandestinely, risking several years in jail if he was caught.

My grandma started talking about the Christmas party in November. "This may be the last *Navidad* we can all get together," she said.

"Next year in Miami" had become her mantra. She invited her brother Armando and his wife, Jacinta, to celebrate with us. Muñeca volunteered to make the roast, the yucca and the dessert. Jacinta would take care of the rice and black beans and Armando, the drinks. Though *Tío* Armando and *Tía* Jacinta were *comecandelas* and often argued with Muñeca over politics, they agreed to come. On one condition: they wouldn't be celebrating Christmas, they warned us, but "another anniversary of the revolutionary triumph."

Ponciano, naturally, voted against the idea. "What's the point of having these people over?" he asked Muñeca. "They don't care about us."

"They are *family*, Poncianito."

"Family, *merde*! Don't count on me for that stupid party. I'm not staying."

"I already knew that."

He always went to the Capablanca Chess Club on Christmas Eve. The only places that Ponciano visited regularly were the cemetery, the restaurants where he worked as a *colero*, and the chess club. Ma mère said he was an avid player but I never saw a chess set at home.

In the end, as usual, Muñeca prevailed. Arrangements for the *fiesta de Navidad* began. But there were problems right away. The motor of our refrigerator, an aged Frigidaire, stopped working. A clandestine mechanic charged two hundred pesos to repair it. "The party is doomed," Ponciano said, taking off his eyeglasses. His green eyes had an evil, *mal agüero* gleam.

The trip to Pinar del Río took around five hours. Papucho and Gerardo left the Havana Train Station on a Saturday morning. They were supposed to come back the following evening with the slaughtered pig hidden in unmarked suitcases. If the police stopped them, they could claim they had just found the suitcases and didn't know what was inside. A feeble excuse, but an excuse nonetheless...

The next day Ma mère and I went to pick them up in a '55 Chevy that Fernando, a family friend, rented to us in exchange for three pounds of pork. This was also an underground business since taxi drivers were only allowed to work for the state.

The Pinar del Río train arrived on time but Papucho and Gerardo didn't. There wasn't another train from Piloto until Tuesday. We went home and waited for a phone call explaining the delay. Yet the days passed and no one called. Ma mère began to get anxious. Papucho was carrying eight hundred pesos, four times his monthly salary.

"You should have gone with him," Muñeca told her. "He has enough money to buy two barrels of Coronilla rum."

"But he hasn't drunk since we applied for the exit

permits," my mother replied.

"Which means he'll go on the biggest drinking binge of his life," Ponciano put in. "The guy now has a three-month old thirst."

"Oh, he'll be so ashamed if...," Ma mère started to say.

"Don't be so naïve, Carmencita!" Muñeca cut her off. "That husband of yours doesn't have one ounce of shame."

My trust in Papucho began to fail. *La otra*, a disciple of Ponciano, had no faith at all. And when Gerardo's wife joined Ma mère and me at the train station, her comments were everything but soothing.

"Gerardo drank in just one day the two bottles of rum we got by the ration card," she admitted.

"*Ay*, Alicia, don't tell me that, *por Dios*!" Ma mère exclaimed.

But Papucho wouldn't drink *too much* during Christmas. He prided himself in staying sober, or semi-sober, while the regular non-drinkers had a couple of beers and made fools out of themselves. He laughed at the unskilled drunks who, after a glass of rum, tried to sing the Spanish version of White Christmas, *Blanca Navidad*, so out of tune that it ended up being a sad mockery, *triste Navidad*.

"I'll never get drunk after the tenth of December," he had said many times. "That's for beginners."

It was December fifteenth. And he had promised not to touch another drop of alcohol, hadn't he? But Muñeca suspected that it wouldn't take long to change Papucho's mind, particularly when he had an encouraging companion and plenty of pesos in his pocket. "I'm afraid we aren't going to see that pig's ears," she said.

The Tuesday train was crowded but Papucho and Gerardo weren't among the passengers. By then we owed

Fernando six pounds of pork or their equivalent, eighty pesos. He was getting anxious too.

There was little we could do. The *guajiro* Miguel didn't have a phone. Telegrams took a week to get to Piloto and the service wasn't reliable. Calling the police could get Papucho and Gerardo in trouble if they were found with "incriminating evidence," that is, with a dead pig in their suitcases.

"Didn't I say that the party was doomed?" Ponciano gloated.

After another trip to the train station, Ma mère cried, lit a candle in front of her Virgin of Charity altar and prayed for Papucho's return. "Dear Oshún," she said, addressing the virgin by her *orisha* name, "Please bring my husband back. Though he's a drunk and rather lazy, I love him."

"But he doesn't drink every day," I hurried to explain, not wanting the virgin to get the wrong idea about my father.

Papucho had never spent a night in the streets nor stayed out for so long. We called his mother, Grandma Rosa, but she hadn't heard from him either. Where was he? I asked *la otra* and wrote an urgent letter to Fidel, placed carefully in my Aniuska doll, but got no response from either one.

Three more days passed. In the meantime, Alicia got news. Gerardo had been spotted in the Piloto streets, drunk out of his skull and accompanied by another *borracho*. My mother was so angry at Papucho that she even talked of divorcing him. Muñeca agreed. "I've never understood what you saw in that drunkard," she said. "You could have married a more successful man. More educated. More...like you."

"I'm afraid you're right," Ma mère answered, looking down. "But I've tried all these years. I've kept hoping..."

"There is nothing to hope for, *hija*! He's a *borracho* and will die a *borracho*. Just face it."

"You're right," Ma mère repeated. "And I'm getting tired, you know?"

That was, I recognized later, the beginning of the end.

§ § §

A fourth, unsuccessful trip to the train station took place. My mother, looking tired and depressed, said that we needed to take a bus this time because there might not be any pork to pay Fernando. She had lost her faith too.

On our way back, after we got off at the Alameda Movie Theater, a man ran after us. He had thinning hair, elephant-like ears and a warm smile. "Carmen! Carmita!" he called to my mother. "Do you remember me?"

"Humberto Orozco!" her face changed instantly and became rosier. "Where have you been?"

I had heard his name at home. Humberto Orozco and Ma mère had been high school sweethearts. In 1958 he left her, and his own "bourgeois" family, to join *El Comandante* in the Sierra Maestra Mountains. My mother went to college and, years later, married Papucho. Orozco married a *rebelde* comrade and became a doctor. He was a prominent *comecandela*. Ma mère had heard about him through common friends but they hadn't met again.

"In Angola, for the last three years," he answered.

"What did you do there?"

"I was an international doctor. Now I work at a polyclinic here in Lawton, on San Mariano Street."

"Well, I live at the corner of San Anastasio and San Mariano streets."

"I know, *chica*. I still remember the way to your house," Ma mère blushed and he went on, "We are neighbors because I spend more time at the polyclinic than at home. I'm a volunteer *miliciano*, too."

"Ah."

"I've been asking everybody about you, Carmita. What have you been doing these years?"

"I work for *Revista Mujeres*. I'm an editor there."

"You always had a way with words. But I thought you and your folks had gone to Miami a long time ago. It's a pity that our political ideas aren't the same."

Ma mère changed the subject, tactfully, "*Mira*, this is my daughter, Longina."

"Oh—you got married. Well, Longina looks very intelligent. Just like you."

"Thanks," I said, feeling an instant sympathy for someone who didn't come up with the "what a pretty girl" cliché that most adults spat. I knew I wasn't pretty and fake compliments made me sulk.

Doctor Orozco and Ma mère talked nonstop for a good hour. After his return from Angola he had been given a Lada, a Soviet car, as a reward. He offered to take us home, but we refused since it was only a few blocks away.

"I will drop by your house one of these days, Carmita, if your husband doesn't mind it," he said, bashfully.

"You are welcome anytime. And Muñeca will be enchanted to see you again."

Ma mère was humming *Se fue* all the way home.

The following evening Doctor Orozco came and took her out.

"We are going to visit several hospitals," Ma mère explained to me, "in case your father had an accident and is unable to call us."

She smelled of her favorite fragrance that was, until her political ideas took a turn to the left, Chanel N°5. She had bought it on the black market and wore it only on special occasions. But this was a regular weekday and she was supposed to be concerned about Papucho, no? The whiff of sophistication that filled the house seemed out of place.

When Muñeca saw Ma mère get in Doctor Orozco's Lada, she smiled knowingly and began to sing *Lágrimas Negras*, an old ballad by the Trío Matamoros,

Un jardinero de amor
Siembra una flor y se va.
Otro viene y la cultiva.
¿De cuál de los dos será?
(A gardener of love
Plants a flower and leaves.
Another one tends to it.
To whom will it belong?)

I didn't like the not-too-subtle message. Would that big-eared guy have the intention of taking Papucho's place? As if reading my mind, Muñeca said, "I think Carmita has just found a *replacement*."

"Like you found Ramoncito," I replied, almost aggressively.

She stared at me, shocked, "*Niña*! You are getting too big for your britches. You are becoming a *cabroncita*, you know?"

A *cabrón* is a bastard. But a *cabroncita*, at least in my grandma's vocabulary, was a pretty smart ass.

"I don't want Papucho to be replaced!" I said and left the room in tears.

A remorseful Muñeca rushed to console me.

"Don't worry," she said. "Papucho will come home. Where is he going to go that he's worth more? And your mother will forgive him. She always does. I was just joking. *Anda*, let's watch together Nitza Villapol's show."

Nitza Villapol had a cooking show on Channel 6—*Cocina al Minuto*, that is, Cooking to Order or Cooking in Minutes. The latter was a more appropriate name because we lacked so many ingredients that making dinner didn't take a long time. Nitza's show had started in the early fifties and Muñeca commented how her recipes had changed after 1959. They went from olive-garnished chicken and rice and minced meat with onions and raisins to cucumber lemonade and cheeseless macaroni. Now Nitza warned her audience that eating too much beef was unhealthy. That sounded funny since we got only one pound of red meat per person each month.

My grandma accused Nitza of being a government brownnoser. But because she came up with useful recipes, Muñeca would sit in front of the TV, notebook and pen in hand, to copy them. As soon as I learned to write she entrusted me with this task. In a few months we had our own *Cocina al Minuto* cookbook at home. But Nitza's peculiar desserts, like beets boiled with brown sugar, never tempted my appetite.

The hospital search was useless. The next morning Ma mère, advised by Doctor Orozco, decided to alert the police. But when she opened the door, cursing "that damned *borracho*," she saw him. He was sitting on our porch floor with a week-old beard, a bruised face and no suitcases in sight. "Are you hurt, Papucho?" she cried out. "Are you sick? Are you drunk?"

He mumbled "yes" three times and crawled into the house under Muñeca's disapproving gaze.

I felt cheated, to say the least. Not only had Papucho broken his promise, but he had also ruined our Christmas party. Muñeca was right. He didn't have one ounce of shame.

It turned out that Miguel had lost all his pigs that year due to an epidemic. The few Piloto peasants who had animals left didn't want to sell them. So Papucho and Gerardo partied without remorse, spending their days in seedy bars and sleeping in alleys. They got into a fight with a thug who tried to steal their wallets and gave Papucho a bloody lip. The suitcases were lost after the confrontation. "But they were empty," my father assured us. He caught a cold after lying for hours, passed out, on the wet grass of Piloto Central Park. With their last fifty pesos the smashed *compadres* took the Havana train, coughing and feverish, and bought a bottle of cheap Coronilla rum "to keep their bones warm."

Ma mère nursed Papucho's wounds. And he, looking embarrassed and sorry, promised her solemnly, "I will not touch another drop of alcohol for the rest of my life, *mi amor*."

Muñeca and Ponciano said "Ha." I couldn't help but being of the same mind. I wouldn't trust adults—or anybody—again.

Alicia blamed my father for leading her husband astray. Ma mère, offended, replied that "poor Papucho" had never drunk during Christmas until he went out with Gerardo. Muñeca sided with Alicia. A monumental fight ensued and that was the end of our pig-buying venture.

We didn't have any pork to cook or contacts to buy another in time for Christmas. The party was cancelled. *Tío* Armando and *Tía* Jacinta, believing that Muñeca had cheated her way out of the celebration, didn't talk to her for months. Ma mère had to pay Fernando a hundred pesos for the three useless rides to the train station. We ate only rice, beans and chicken croquettes that *triste Navidad.*

The next year Papucho resumed his drinking. Muñeca continued badmouthing him. Life went on as before. Except for Doctor Orozco's visits which became more and more frequent with every month that passed.

§ § §

The failed Christmas party was followed by a series of misfortunes. First, our petition to leave was rejected. In the telegram sent by an emigration officer, we were ordered to stay in Cuba. "The *núcleo familiar* isn't allowed to leave." Period. Muñeca put the blame on Ponciano's knack for *mal agüero*. "But I am not going to give up!" she yelled. "I will go to Miami again, despite Castro, Ponciano and the *orishas* themselves!"

I thought that *El Comandante* had read my letter and personally denied the exit permits, and I felt guilty. But *la otra* was content.

"Papucho would drink himself to death in *La Yuma*," she told me. "Don't you know that rum can be bought there without coupons?"

The denial of the exit permits had troublesome consequences. The president of our Committee for the Defense of the Revolution, Barbarita, and those who sang *La Internacional* during Red Sundays shunned us. Ma mère lost her job at *Revista Mujeres*, a magazine that appealed to a revolutionary readership. She was transferred to a clothing factory where the other employees, who were *comecandelas*, made her life miserable and called her *La Gusana*. My father was sent to build latrines at the *Mártires de Playa Girón* labor camp. It was so far from Lawton that he had to wake up at four A.M. to be there at eight.

At school, *Maestra* Mercedes and the principal insisted on cleaning the ideological mess my family had made. I had to read *The Pioneers' Manual* and answer endless questions about it. I had to sing loudly and clearly the *Hymn of the Heroic Guerrilla* and other revolutionary songs during the morning civic acts. I was assigned a "mentor" named Catalina, a young teacher whose mission was to lead me back to *El Comandante*'s path and monitor me.

"Are your parents still thinking of going to the United States?" Catalina would ask me from time to time.

But I had been instructed by Muñeca on what to say and answered with my best Pioneer smile. "Not at all, comrade! They got that silly idea out of their heads. They are good revolutionaries now."

Catalina looked doubtful and often searched my backpack. What did she expect to find? A request for another exit permit? A Christmas postcard? A letter from the CIA?

My grandparents suffered less because they weren't in close contact with overzealous colleagues. However, the *gusano* mark branded them too. The butcher and the grocery store clerks gave them the worst portions and told them to shop in Miami if they wanted something better. They had been classified as counterrevolutionary at the beginning of the exit process. Now everybody in the neighborhood knew they didn't like the system but they couldn't go anywhere.

A week after the petitions to leave were rejected, *Celia Cruz* knocked at our door at seven-thirty in the morning. "Guess what came to the hardware store for the C-45 coupon," the *colera* told my grandma, gasping. "Alarm clocks again. You are lucky!"

This time Muñeca ran to the store without combing her hair or even changing her checkered dressing gown.

But our troubles weren't over. First Papucho was thrown in jail. Then, while he was away, a hurricane hit us. It crushed trees, destroyed houses and brought back Doña Lola's ghost.

Chapter 4

A tropical storm starts with a lower, indigo horizon and a subtle smell of rain in the air.

Hours later, big raindrops beat the roofs as if dancing the mambo to the wild drums of thunder. *Tumbaquín.* Glasses, vases and mirrors are shattered. Shouts, prayers and curses are carried by the wind. Dogs howl. And there is always someone who turns on a battery radio to add rumba to the chaos. *Tumbaquín.* Waves slap the shore in an incessant, chronometrical motion. Buildings crumble. *Tumbaquín.* Nights become dull and colorless because of the blackouts. . .

But blackouts, *apagones*, weren't always caused by hurricanes. During the sugarcane harvest period we had several every month because energy was saved for sugar production. At eight P.M., when the broadcast of the evening news was about to start, or in the middle of a soap opera, a dark cellophane curtain suddenly enveloped the house. It was *el apagón.*

The TV fell silent, to my grateful relief. I loathed political harangues and military marches. The high-pitched wailing of soap-opera heroines grated on my nerves. During blackouts, the only audible sounds at home were the chanting of crickets and Muñeca's soft voice, whispering *Se fue.* For the quiet child I was, *el apagón* was a gift from the Magi.

Next door, Tony played the violin. The fluid melody sounded eerie in the silence that covered San Anastasio Street. It was during one of those romantic blackout nights that Carlitos had asked me if I wanted to be his girlfriend. This was another reason why I loved *el apagón.*

§ § §

Havana braced for a category-four storm. It had been raining for two days. Old buildings in La Habana Vieja had been evacuated. Hospitals sent patients home. Stores, offices and schools closed. We had no electricity, but I knew that it wasn't an ordinary blackout. Nothing was ordinary, in fact. Ma mère was sleeping alone, on the living room sofa. Papucho wasn't home. Muñeca and Ponciano acted in an odd, secretive manner and didn't seem to want me around.

"Why don't you go play with Carlitos and Sandra?" my grandma asked me every day after lunch. And she herself took me to our neighbors' house, holding an old pink umbrella, like a withered rose, over our heads.

Ponciano whispered. Ma mère tiptoed. And I wondered what was going on, though I suspected it had something to do with my father's absence. Muñeca had told me that Papucho was spending a few weeks with his mother. Grandma Rosa lived in Los Pinos, a distant suburb, and we seldom visited her. But I knew better. Papucho was in jail. Carlitos had overheard Rita and Silvana as they gossiped about it.

When the hurricane season began, Papucho had tried to buy cement and bricks at a Lawton store, but was told that construction materials wouldn't "come" until the following year. Then he quietly stole them from the *Mártires de Playa Girón* camp. His coworkers didn't mind it—they were stealing too—but a *chivato*, a neighborhood informer, noticed that he was repairing the house and denounced us. My father was sentenced to one month in jail for "diversion of resources."

I was proud of him. Before the repairs our ceiling was ready to collapse. When it rained, all the buckets we had were unable to contain the leaks. Muñeca resorted to pots, kettles and bowls strategically placed to collect the water. On desperate occasions, Ponciano's urinal was also called to duty.

Papucho had taken care of all that. "We have a terrific father," *la otra* bragged, which made me think she considered herself my sister or something similar. I also thought she had forgotten that Papucho was "a lazy, good-for-nothing drunk." But now, despite Papucho's efforts, the ceiling was getting swollen again with all the rain it had absorbed and water trickled down the walls.

"Help us, *Dios Padre, Virgen del Carmen, Virgen del Cobre* and *San* Millán de la Cogolla!" Ma mère cried out as the first gusts made the house quiver.

When worried, she invoked all the members of the heavenly court. She usually started with God the Father, followed with several virgins and finished with *San* Millán de la Cogolla, an obscure Spanish hermit that few people in Cuba prayed to.

Ponciano put a plank behind the front door. Muñeca and Ma mère nailed the windows and stuffed their splintering frames with old newspapers. Tony and Silvana were also busy securing doors and windows. Carlitos teased his sister. Silvana scolded him. Their voices could be heard over the wind's howls.

"Let's have the boat ready in case we need to evacuate," Tony said.

That was a joke. Common people couldn't own boats. They were illegal items, like pigs and Christmas trees.

"If the waters get high enough, we'll float to the Malecón. And from there, to *La Yuma*!" he went on.

"*Tía* Rita's nightgown will make a good sail," Carlitos chuckled.

"And your bony legs can double as oars, *Gato Flaco*!" Rita shot back.

Rita was so big and fat that Carlitos called her Her Immenseness. She took it in stride and nicknamed him Scrawny Cat. I liked her. Rita made great pumpkin custard and added raisins when available. She didn't follow Nitza Villapol's recipes!

The rain got heavier. It sounded as if ten Ritas were dancing rumba on our frail roof. Dirty water came out of a toilet, forming a foul lagoon in the hall. A cascade fell on the kitchen counter. "Thank God it wasn't over the Frigidaire," Muñeca groaned.

Luckily our neighbor Luisito happened to pass by and helped us make the house safe. He put boards over the windows to protect the glasses and brought candles, bottled water and five pounds of black beans. Luisito was a handsome young man, courteous, obliging, sweet and very, very effeminate. His parents had gone to *La Yuma* in 1978 but Luisito, being of draft age, wasn't allowed to follow them. Muñeca took him under her wing and became his surrogate mother. "He's never shown any carnal interest in me," she would say in a surprised tone, as if talking about an inconceivable fact.

The situation was black with gray hemstitches. The only pink note in that gloomy landscape was a package that my grandmother's sister had sent from Miami a week before. I waited for it impatiently after hearing that it contained not only clothes and medicine but also toys for me.

The Magi, *los Reyes Magos* who used to bring gifts to children on the sixth of January, didn't come anymore. Muñeca said the Three Kings were in exile too. Since the early seventies, toys were distributed through the ration card. Kids under the age of twelve had the right to buy three toys per year. Some had been sent by our partners in the construction of socialism, as *El Comandante* said in his speeches. These were Chinese dollhouses, Czech tricycles and the coveted German electric trains. But most of us only got Soviet dolls, footballs and plastic soldiers. The dolls had rigid blonde hair and names like Aniuska or Sashenka that were later passed on to unfortunate girls.

Muñeca's sister said that she had sent me a Teddy bear and a Barbie doll. Barbie meant Barbarita, Ma mère explained. I thought of the Vigilance commissary with the prominent *culo* and figured that the American doll had a big rump as well. And would she bring her pretty *Yuma* clothes?

While I was lost in Barbie dreams, the hurricane struck Havana. *Tumbaquín*. San Anastasio Street became a kaleidoscope of broken bottles, spinning leaves, levitating zinc roofs and gravity-defying doors. *Ay*, the barking of dogs, the cries of people, and the music from radios and loudspeakers that played the national anthem and revolutionary marches like *26 de Julio* and *La Internacional* in the middle of pandemonium. The shattered mirror in the bathroom—seven years of bad luck, my grandma shuddered—and the wind banging on the door...

I had been ordered to stay in my room. "The hall is slippery and dirty," Muñeca said. "I'll call you when everything is clean."

Being alone while a hurricane raged outside was no fun. Lightning flashes zigzagged across the sky. The *tumbaquín* of thunder grew louder. To make things worse, my room stank. In fact, the entire house did because of the flooded toilet. And it was dark because we had no electricity yet. "Let's ask Muñeca for chamomile tea," *la otra* suggested.

We sneaked out. Ma mère, Ponciano and Muñeca had gathered in the living room. That looked like a family meeting. Were they talking about Papucho's release? I approached softly, hoping to listen to their conversation. But then I felt an urgent, ill-timed need to pee.

The main bathroom was still swamped. Turds and urine covered the floor. Holding my nose, I walked to my parents' room. A smaller bathroom could be accessed through it. I opened the bedroom door and entered. It was humid and dim. I sensed a presence, though I couldn't see anything.

"Hello," I said. "Papucho?"

A woman who had been lying on my parents' bed stirred. She got up and came so close to me that I smelled her acrid breath. In the glow of a lightning flash, I noticed the big, hairy mole on her right cheek.

"Doña Lola!"

She caressed my face. Her fingers had the texture of the leather that covered Ponciano's books.

"*Oh, mi aldea,*" she shrieked, "*cuánto el alma se recrea al volverte a contemplar.*"

I backed off.

"Have you seen my manuscript?" she asked, this time in a hoarse voice. "I write poetry, hear?"

"Longina, where are you?" Muñeca called.

I slammed the door closed and ran to the kitchen, shaking. The sour taste of vomit had risen to my throat.

"I was in—in the backyard," I stammered, struggling not to *gua* right there. "I wanted to pee but the bathroom looks awful."

She handed me an empty glass bottle, "Go to your room and use this as a urinal. And don't come out again!"

I was so frightened that I peed all over the floor while thunder roared. *Tumbaquín.*

The next day a cerulean sky replaced the overcast horizon. All the soaked earth's aromas came from the backyard. The stench vanished. Ma mère lit a candle in front of her Virgin of Charity altar and thanked Oshún, God the Father and *San* Millán de la Cogolla. The ceiling had resisted. We had survived. Not unscathed, though. The leaks reappeared and the flooded toilets couldn't be used for weeks. Our rations of meat, rice, sugar, beans and soap shrank even more.

A week later I mustered enough courage to bring up the forbidden topic. I went to the kitchen where Muñeca was making cheeseless macaroni and asked, "When did you say my great-grandmother died?"

"Six months before your birth, exactly," she answered.

"Are you sure?"

"Are you going to start again with the *matraquilla*?" she snapped. *Matraquilla* is the same old song.

"And what happened to her book?"

"Which book?"

"Her manuscript. The poetry book she wrote."

"Ponciano has it. Or it got lost. I don't know and I don't care. Why don't you just forget it? I've told you a hundred times that curiosity killed the cat."

I left the kitchen convinced that I had seen my great-grandmother's spirit, who wanted to recover her poetry book. But *la otra*, always quite contrary, replied that Doña Lola was alive and well, and that we had seen no ghost. "Spirits do not have bad breath, *chica*," she said. "*No jodas*!"

That night I took a piece of paper and sat down to write a letter to *El Comandante*.

Dear Fidel,

Thanks for keeping us safe. I saw in the news that many people lost their homes. Thanks for the package with *la* Barbie, too. I hope it arrives soon. And please, *Comandante*, forgive my father for not being a good comrade. He didn't steal the cement with bad intentions. Free him soon, hear? We need him.

Revolutionarily,

Longina

But Papucho had to serve his entire sentence. He came back skinny and embittered, swearing eternal wrath to informers and *comecandelas*. He resumed drinking, too, and *Ma mere* threatened with divorce again.

In vain I looked for Doña Lola's manuscript. I searched my parents' room, the kitchen, the library and even the backyard. Once I asked Ponciano about it and he told me to go to *casa del carajo*—literally, to hell. But I knew the book would appear someday. And it certainly did, several years later and in the middle of a different, worse kind of storm.

We never got the Miami package. By a government decree, all parcels sent from *La Yuma* were passed from the *gusanos* for whom they were intended to the victims of the hurricane. *Au revoir*, Barbie! *Adiós*, Teddy bear! They vanished in a tornado of flying leaves and broken bottles. I could only conjure them up during the black-out nights, among the chanting of the crickets and the acrobatics of fireflies.

Chapter 5

With the advent of fall a magic carpet of brown, red and yellow leaves landed on the backyard. I loved to walk barefoot on the soft cushion despite the centipedes and lizards that nestled in the grass. The air smelled different, pregnant with the fragrance of the jasmines and roses that would be withered in a few weeks. There was also the musky smell of smoke. Though it was forbidden, a few neighbors would burn their trash at night.

It cooled off by the end of September. No one missed the humid July heat or the implacable August sun. We weren't covered in sweat most of the day. Around Malecón Drive, tall waves hit the seawall. Revolutionary marches and calls for voluntary work diminished. Fall was a pleasant season. It was also when more people tried to reach *La Yuma*, fleeing the island on homemade rafts.

"What's going on with Tony and Silvana?" Muñeca asked Ponciano. "I haven't seen them in a while, have you?"

"They are probably minding their own business," he replied with a yawn.

Our neighbors kept to themselves and appeared to avoid us. Rita didn't sit on the front porch to knit anymore and I hadn't played with Carlitos and Sandra in a whole month.

"I wonder if they are mad at us," she insisted. "You haven't said anything impertinent to them, I hope."

He didn't bother to answer. Muñeca then tiptoed to the backyard. Only a small concrete wall separated the two houses. I followed her, my feet sinking in a thick, gaudy layer of leaves. Tony's backyard was a mess. Planks of wood, truck tires and bolts were scattered all over. It looked like a junkyard, but a couple of oars hidden among the weeds gave them away. "They are building a boat!" my grandma said.

"What for?" I asked.

"To leave the country, *niña*. To go to *El Norte*," she answered. "It doesn't surprise me. I've always known that Tony and Silvana didn't like 'this.'"

"This" meant the revolution and its consequences: nationalization of private business, scarcity of food, medicine and clothes, prohibition of travel. . . It was a term used only by those who disagreed with the government. Its supporters, like Barbarita and Doctor Orozco, said "*la revolución*."

A few days later Tony told my parents about his plans. Perhaps he figured out that they already knew. He showed his work-in-progress to Papucho saying with pride, "This is my magnum opus, mate."

Tony had a degree in Philosophy. Before "this," he had been a professor at a private college, the University of Villanueva. When it was closed by *la revolución*, he became a high school teacher. He played the violin in the evenings and cards on Saturday nights. Ofelia, the president of the local Committee for the Defense of the Revolution, said he suffered from "ideological weakness" and the *comecandelas* kept an eye on him.

Since they knew we were *gusanos* too, Tony and his wife tried to convince my parents to go with them. "It's only ninety miles from here to Key West," Silvana said. "Around the corner, *vaya*."

"Some people make it in less than two days," Tony added.

"Well, if we had a compass...,"Papucho started to say.

But Ma mère wouldn't hear of it, "I'd rather die of

hunger in Cuba than be swallowed by a shark. Forget it!"

Tony's "magnum opus" looked fragile and awkward, like an oversized bathtub. I couldn't imagine how five people, among them Her Immenseness, would fit in it.

"They are nuts," Ma mère said when we returned home.

"Taking the children isn't a good idea," Muñeca agreed. "Tony should go by himself and claim his family later."

"They all will die at sea...," Ponciano prophesied. He had joined the discussion as soon as it took a tragic tone.

"*Ay*, shut up!" Muñeca crossed herself. "Don't bring these people your *mal agüero*, please."

"...That is, supposing the Vigilance patrol doesn't catch them before," Ponciano went on, unusually animated. "Stop going to their house and talking to them, hear? Sooner or later an informer will find out and *we* will be in trouble too. Remember what Thomas à Kempis said, '*Many a time I wished that I had held my peace and had not associated with men.*'"

Muñeca rolled her eyes.

My grandfather felt a special fondness for the *Imitation of Christ*. He wasn't Catholic or even religious but quoted *el* Kempis, as we called it, every time he had a chance. Muñeca maintained that this was just another sign of neurasthenia because the book was indigestible.

At eight years of age I preferred to read adult stuff. I found children's books, particularly Soviet translations like *Stories and Paintings* and *Blue Leaves*, too short, too simple and too dull. But I couldn't make sense of *el* Kempis. The Christian references lost me. Its pages were as thin as onionskin and the font, irritatingly small. "Handwriting of fleas," Muñeca said. She had predicted that reading so much would ruin my eyesight and my brain.

"*La niña* is going to end up a blind, antisocial library mouse," she warned my parents. "Why don't you get rid of those old books? All they do is gather dust."

Her suggestion always brought up indignant protests from Ma mère and Ponciano. But Muñeca was right, at least about my loss of vision. I began wearing eyeglasses when I was six years old.

I would have left *el* Kempis alone but Doctor Orozco once told me that it was an "ideologically deviant book." Whatever that was, "ideologically deviant" sounded enticing enough. I went back to *el* Kempis with renovated interest. I also hoped to find some useful information there about the existence of spirits, since I hadn't forgotten Doña Lola's visit.

What would Doctor Orozco have said, had he known I was reading George Orwell's *Animal Farm* too? Ma mère had explained to me what each character represented. Comparing *El Comandante* with Napoleon, the head pig, seemed quite disrespectful and "ideologically deviant" indeed.

One night while my mother and Muñeca were at Silvana's house, another neighbor showed up. It was Barbarita, the Vigilance commissary who had given me Fidel's calendar, the most ardent *comecandela* in San Anastasio Street. "*Hola*, my friends," she purred. "May I come in?"

That was an unexpected call. Barbarita had criticized the family before because they avoided participation in Red Sundays, went to church and displayed Christmas lights at home. But there she was, all smiles, carrying a dish of rice pudding. "It's for Rita," she told Silvana. "I know that your sister loves *arroz con leche.*"

She joined the group. The others were clearly uncomfortable and kept quiet for a while. But when my grandma mentioned Ofelia's last call for voluntary work, Barbarita exploded,

"*La* Ofelia! Uff! I can't stand her anymore. She is a fanatic. And people need to be more understanding. Not everyone likes 'this.' As a matter of fact, 'this' isn't for everyone." Barbarita lowered her voice, "I am not even sure that 'this' is for me anymore. All I hear is, 'Comrade Bárbara, cut cane. Comrade Bárbara, plant coffee.' But the grocery store is empty. So is the *panadería*. It's not easy!"

"Who would ever believe that in this country, where sugarcane grows everywhere, people could buy only six pounds of sugar per month?" Muñeca asked.

"Boys are drafted at eighteen and military service is compulsory," Silvana sighed.

"Kids have to work at labor camps as soon as they start middle school. Even the girls."

The more our neighbors and Muñeca talked, the edgier Ma mère appeared. Her face had become what Papucho called "*cara de tranca*." When she got mad, my mother looked as if she wanted to grab a stick, a *tranca*, and hit someone with it. She left soon, dragging my grandma with her.

I scurried to the backyard and found Carlitos building a toy raft. Because he was "a man in training," Carlitos knew of his parents' plans. He also knew he shouldn't talk about them. But I was his girlfriend.

"Will you visit me in *La Yuma*?" he whispered, running his fingers through my hair.

"I'm afraid that *El Comandante* won't allow it," I said. "He didn't let us go when we asked for exit permits."

"That's why dad wants to do it in secret."

"But my grandfather says you can be caught."

"So? It's easier to ask for forgiveness than permission."

Sandra came prancing. "Barbarita's *arroz con leche* was awesome!" she said.

We took Carlitos's toy ships to a wooden tub where Silvana washed their clothes. At home we had an American washing machine, but Silvana was a *guajira*, a peasant from Oriente who did house chores in the old fashioned way. She swept with a broom made out of twigs and cooked with wood instead of gas. In her immaculate kitchen the burning embers looked like fireflies scattered over the oven.

Carlitos was the captain of a pirate ship and attacked our fishing boats.

"That's not fair!" Sandra cried when he sank my boat and hers. "We were the *good* ones!"

"Villains always win in the end," her brother explained. "Haven't you watched any movies, *eh*?"

Sandra ran to her room wailing. Carlitos and I tossed handfuls of red and yellow leaves at each other. They looked like the confetti people threw over newlyweds. Inside the house, Tony played *Les feuilles morts* on his violin while Barbarita, Silvana and Rita chatted away in the living room.

When I came home, my folks were busy dissecting Barbarita's shocking statements.

"She knows Tony and Silvana are leaving and wants to join them because she is disillusioned with 'this,'" Muñeca said. "Why don't we go too?"

"Don't talk nonsense!" Ma mère huffed. "That crappy boat won't even make it to the town of Regla. And Barbarita has belonged to the Vigilance patrol for years. How come she's suddenly turned into a *gusana*?"

"Remember all the nasty things she called us when we applied for the exit permits, though it was all legal," Papucho said.

Ponciano repeated his favorite motto, "You can't trust anyone. Havana is plagued by *informateurs*."

He never said *chivatos*, favoring the French term.

"Barbarita used to be a hard-nosed communist, but that doesn't make her a bad person," Muñeca said. "She might have had a change of heart."

"A change of *culo* is what she's had!" my father replied. "I bet she hides two pillows under those tight pants to make guys believe that she has a bigger butt."

He began to whistle *La Engañadora* (The Cheater) a chacha song about a girl who did just that.

A Prado y Neptuno iba una chiquita
Que todos los hombres la tenían que mirar.
Estaba gordita y bien formadita
En resumen, colosal.
(A girl used to go to Prado and Neptuno
All the guys had to take a look at her.
She was plump and well shaped
In sum, a gorgeous girl.)

Muñeca grabbed Ponciano and tried to make him dance.

Pero todo en esta vida se sabe
Sin siquiera averiguar.
Se ha sabido que en sus formas
Relleno tan sólo hay.
(But everything in life is found out
Without even prying too much.
We have learned that her curves
Are just padding.)

She mimicked the actions, swinging her own (and

definitely genuine) ass. Papucho and Ponciano laughed and hooted. But then my mother noticed me and turned *cara de tranca* again.

"Why are you always around when we talk about grown-up matters?" she asked. "Go to your room and entertain yourself with your dollhouse, or go to bed."

"Give me *el* Kempis," I said.

"It's in the reading room. *Anda*!"

"You are too prissy, Carmen," I heard Muñeca say as I left. "Don't you know that *la niña* learns worse things at school?"

"It may very well be, but I don't want you putting ideas in her head *here*," Ma mère replied.

I ran to my bedroom and hid a small pillow under my panties. Then I marched to the reading room, swinging the best I could my new and improved *culito* to the beat of *La Engañadora*.

§ § §

By mid October the boat was completed to Tony's satisfaction. He would get in it with Silvana, Rita and the kids and practice "rowing" among the weeds. They bought lifesavers, plastic containers to carry water and all the canned food they could get on the black market. The trip seemed inevitable.

"I'll send for you soon," Carlitos promised, kissing me on the lips as lovers did in *La Yuma* movies. "We'll reach Miami in less than two days!"

He looked so happy that I couldn't help feeling hurt. I had secretly hoped that he wanted to stay with me, or at least that he said so.

"*Au revoir*," I said coldly. Then I jumped the wall and went home.

"That's how men are," *la otra* told me when I complained. "You can't trust them. Actually, you can't trust anyone."

I realized that *la otra* repeated many of Ponciano's phrases. Could she be *his* imaginary pal too?

I retreated to the reading room to mourn. And, as usual, the sight of all those books made me forget my troubles. Five oak shelves contained the Encyclopedia Britannica, a world Atlas, several dictionaries, the complete works of Flaubert and Zola (in French, naturally), Valle-Inclán, Cervantes, Pérez Galdós... On the walls were a marina painted by Leopoldo Romañach, the portrait of a young Ponciano and a Mona Lisa reproduction.

"Notice her eyes," Ponciano once pointed out. "They follow you anywhere you go. If you damage a book, spit or do something improper here, Mona Lisa will tell me later, hear?"

"Is she an *informateur*?" I asked.

"One never knows who is an *informateur*," he answered, "does one?"

I nodded. I had learned that much.

When everything was ready for their departure, our neighbors threw a secret farewell party. Just a *fiestecita*, as Silvana put it, to which they invited "only a few good friends."

"I'm not going," Ma mère said. "Even Ofelia's cat knows what's going on now. That house will be chock-full of *chivatos*."

The day of the party, she and my grandma were seated on the squeaky rocking chairs of the front porch when Muñeca pointed to Barbarita. The former *com-*

ecandela crossed San Anastasio Street carrying another dish of rice pudding.

"I smell a rat here," she said.

Barbarita had her tightest red pants on. A puzzling Mona Lisa smile curved her lips when she knocked at Tony's door.

Ma mère came in, shaking her head. Muñeca stayed outside until seven-thirty pretending shc was sweeping the porch, but actually keeping an eye on our neighbor's house.

Silvana's party ended at nine P.M. with a police raid. From my bedroom I heard the cruisers' sirens and Rita's hysterical cries. At home, Muñeca turned off all the lights. "Don't make any noise," she whispered. "Let's pretend we are asleep."

The wind blew furiously, filling the front porch with broken branches, leaves and small rocks. I began to fear Doña Lola's return. She had a penchant for coming with the rain, didn't she?

"Are ghosts afraid of the police?" I asked Muñeca.

"Hush, *niña*!"

The bell rang. I jumped up and so did Muñeca. She almost fainted when a man in uniform greeted us at the door. But the cop only asked her to take care of Carlitos and Sandra until the morning.

"It'll be a pleasure, comrade," she said, shaking.

My friends, escorted by a police woman, came in looking like political refugees. Papucho took two cots to the reading room and helped them settle in. Muñeca made *café con leche* and my mother brought blankets.

Carlitos and Sandra were huddled together when I approached them with two big glasses full of coffee and milk

"Well, the *La Yuma* trip went belly-up," Carlitos said.

He was pale, but being "a man in training" he tried

to appear nonchalant.

"Why did it go belly-up?" Sandra asked. "And why did these people take *Papi*, *Mami* and *Tía* Rita away?"

"Someone squealed on us," Carlitos answered.

"It was Barbarita," I muttered, trying unsuccessfully to avoid Mona Lisa's stare. "My mother thinks she's a *chivata*."

"Dad was afraid of her, too," Carlitos said. "He told mom and Her Immenseness to be careful but they didn't listen to him."

"But Barbarita brought us *arroz con leche*!" Sandra protested. "And she was always good to me."

"Good people sometimes become villains in the end," Carlitos explained. "Haven't you watched any movies, *eh*?"

Once more, Sandra began to wail. "I don't get it! I just can't understand grown-ups."

"We'll try again," Carlitos told me. "I learned how to build a boat. Miami isn't too far away."

I stuck out my tongue at Mona Lisa and grabbed Ponciano's world Atlas. Carlitos and I poured over it. Yes, *La Yuma* was quite close to Cuba, at least on those thin, dust-smelling pages.

§ § §

All the guests who attended the *fiestecita*, plus the host and hostesses, spent the night in the Lawton police station. The following morning many of them were released after paying a fine. But Tony, Silvana and Rita remained in jail, charged with attempting to leave the country illegally. Silvana's mother came from Oriente to take care of her grandkids.

My folks weren't bothered despite Muñeca's imprudent comments about "this." The *comecandelas* couldn't accuse us of anything. It was already known we were *gusanos* but at least we hadn't tried to flee or gone to the farewell party. We also had Doctor Orozco's protection. While the process against our neighbors took place, he came to visit us in his *miliciano* uniform and driving the blue Lada. Barbarita and Ofelia greeted him with great deference. His presence, more than anything else, helped keep the *comecandelas* at bay.

Hearings were not open to the public but *Celia Cruz*'s daughter was a clerk at the local *Tribunal Revolucionario*. Through her we learned that Barbarita was the main witness against Tony's family. She explained how she had befriended "those counterrevolutionaries" and found out about their plans, which she later transmitted to the political police.

"My daughter said that when Barbarita took the stand, her pants looked ready to burst," *Celia Cruz* told us. "*Qué cochina*! After she has been Tony's neighbor for more than thirty years..."

"Didn't I say you couldn't trust anyone?" Ponciano asked.

Tony's colleagues also testified against him, declaring that he had complained about the education system and refused to take a Marxism seminar and to do voluntary work. He was sentenced to five years in jail and forbidden to teach again. Silvana and Rita got two years of house arrest.

The Vigilance patrol and our Committee for the Defense of the Revolution gave Barbarita a medal in a public act where the *comecandelas* sang *La Internacional*.

A few days later I saw Ponciano counting a stack of pesos in his room. He had taken his eyeglasses off and his eyes glowed like Christmas lights. It occurred to me, for the first time, that money was important. Up to then, the wrinkled bills with José Martí's solemn face and Che Guevara's signature had seemed ugly, greasy and useless. But if Ponciano cared for them that much...

That night I asked Ma mère, "Did Barbarita get a lot of money for squealing on Tony and Silvana?"

"Not at all. Only a tin medal."

"Most informers do their work for free," Papucho said bitterly. "Like the guy who denounced me when I was repairing the house. This *cabrón* country! I wish we could leave, even inside a urinal."

My mother was turning *cara de tranca* again so I retreated to the safety of the reading room. Under Mona Lisa's gaze I opened *el* Kempis and read, *"Do not put your trust in friends and relatives."*

I nodded and started a letter to *El Comandante.*

Dear Fidel,

Carlitos's dad is now in jail. Comrade Barbarita denounced him. Tony is a decent guy. Why did you allow—

I didn't know how to go on. My initial trust in Fidel had been damaged by the *comecandelas*' reaction to our attempt to leave, Papucho's imprisonment and the reading of *Animal Farm*. But having nothing else to replace it with, I had clung to the bearded, almighty image in a state of suspended disbelief. Now Barbarita, the apostle of my faith, had killed it with her betrayal.

The pungent smell of burning wood reached the room. Rita, Carlitos and Sandra were throwing leaves and broken branches in a fire they had built in their backyard. Maybe they were also getting rid of more "incriminating evidence."

I took the calendar and all the letters out of Aniuska's belly. Then I joined our neighbors and asked if I could burn something too.

"Sure, *niña,*" Rita said. "Fire cleanses everything."

I threw calendar and letters in the bonfire and stayed there until the last spark died like the embers in Silvana's kitchen.

The carpet of red, brown and yellow leaves that covered our backyard had lost its magic, turning into a muddy pulp.

Chapter 6

Our house had five rooms, only one working toilet and a constellation of leaks. Spacious but crumbly, it was like a mature woman with a wrinkled face, a sagging *culo*, and a matronly bosom. Muñeca had never liked it, or the neighborhood. She called Lawton "the intestine of Havana" and wanted to move closer to downtown, to a more modern place. She had been nagging Ponciano about it for years. And finally, her dream was close to coming true.

Papucho had worked hard. After the hurricane he had repaired the house again with materials bought on the black market. All the leaks had been masked, all the walls painted. The polished furniture contributed to give a good impression. Our home now looked like a middle-aged lady wearing a reasonable amount of make-up and a well-cut, though worn-out dress. "God and the *orishas* willing, we'll be able to make a good *permuta*," Muñeca said.

A *permuta* is an exchange of houses. In Cuba one can't just sell a house and buy another. One must find someone also in search of a different place to live, a *permutante*, and trade homes. Muñeca had placed herself in charge of the *permuta* operation. Her goal was to get a house in Centro Habana or maybe an apartment in El Vedado, where she had always longed to live.

El Vedado was a chic neighborhood. It was just a step below Miramar, a former "bourgeois" suburb that now belonged to the revolutionary elite. El Vedado houses didn't have American-style lawns, picket fences and swimming pools like the Miramar mansions. But they were comfortable and even luxurious, at least when compared to rundown Lawton buildings. Miramar was out of our range, but El Vedado, though an ambitious target, wasn't.

El Vedado was dotted with hotels like Habana Libre, Capri and Riviera. The Focsa building, the López Serrano and other skyscrapers gave it a faint *La Yuma* look. *Apagones* were scarce there. The best restaurants (La Torre, El Conejito) were located there, as well as Coppelia, the biggest ice cream parlor in the city. And it was close to the seawall drive, *El* Malecón, which guaranteed a constant ocean breeze even during the hottest summer evening.

Centro Habana was less pretentious. The streets were narrow and dirty, though a few large avenues like Carlos III and Belascoaín crossed it. It suffered regular blackouts and there were no fancy hotels or restaurants around. In short, it was *un barrio medio pelo*, a low-middle class 'hood. But *Tío* Armando lived in Centro Habana and assured us that it was a good place to live. "It's going to be remodeled soon," he said. "*La revolución* is doing its best to renovate this area." For *Tío* Armando, *la revolución* was always doing "its best."

La Habana Vieja was the last resort. Many of the colonial houses built in the 18th and 19th centuries had become tenements. When people lacked water to flush the toilets, they simply threw their shit into the streets. The more considerate neighbors wrapped it in the pages of *Granma*, the official newspaper of the Cuban Communist Party, because it was cheap and easy to get. A house in La Habana Vieja wasn't much of an improvement over the one we had.

La Gabita, a *permutante*, walked up and down the hall inspecting everything, from the door frames to the cracked tiles. She seemed unimpressed. "Let's go back to the bathrooms," she said, after examining suspiciously the kitchen ceiling. "Are you sure that the sink can be unplugged?"

Muñeca was concerned. Up to then, nobody had shown any interest in exchanging houses with us though she had been placing *permuta* ads for three months, all over the city. I had my own real estate worries. Did La Gabita know that our home harbored a ghost? Would Doña Lola's presence add to or detract from the value of the property?

La Gabita finally admitted she didn't want our place, but needed it to be part of a chain of moves. She explained her plans to my parents, shaking her pudgy arms adorned with beaded Santería bracelets. "You guys take my house, the other people come here and I get the Centro Habana apartment..."

"Wait a minute!" Muñeca barged in. "We have to see your place first."

"Oh, you are going to *love* it!"

Moving to a ghost-less place sounded like a good idea. But how would I keep in touch with Carlitos and Sandra? They didn't have a phone. Silvana and Rita couldn't take them to visit us. Tony was still in jail. Would our new home be walking distance from San Anastasio Street?

La Gabita owned a house in La Habana Vieja. She was already in negotiations with a family that lived in Centro Habana, right on Carlos III Avenue. They were ten *guajiros*, former peasants from Oriente who had been given their three-bedroom apartment by the government. La Gabita's house, that only had three and half bedrooms, was too small for them. But ours was perfect.

My folks initially agreed to move to La Gabita's. However, a couple of weeks later Muñeca changed her mind. “What’s the point of moving from an old house to *another* old house?” she asked.

She took me to see the Carlos III Avenue apartment. A blue toilet with roses painted on it caught my eye. “An artist used to live here before we did,” the *permutantes* explained, apologetically.

My family decided to deal directly with them. A one-for-one move was arranged but not without protests from La Gabita. Believing that we had taken advantage of her, she insulted Muñeca and threatened to put a Santería curse on us.

The apartment owners were wary about getting into a house built sixty years before. Muñeca offered them a thousand pesos for future repairs, but she didn’t have the entire amount. My parents didn’t either. Part of it had to come from Ponciano’s bank account.

True to his suspicious nature, my grandfather didn’t believe Muñeca had offered that much and called the *permutantes* to make sure she wasn’t pocketing the difference. They took it the wrong way and demanded three thousand pesos. Ponciano sent them to *casa del carajo*. That stalled the negotiations for a couple for months. Finally, the two families reached an agreement and the *permuta* ball began to roll. After several weeks of paperwork, the permission to move was granted by the state. Money discreetly exchanged hands—the Urban Reform laws forbade using cash during a *permuta* transaction—and all the documents were signed.

Our last day in Lawton was a sweltering July morning. Most of the jasmine flowers were gone. The few that still hung from the branches were withered and limp. The asphalt was so hot that my plastic sandals stuck to it. My eyes were burning too because I had been crying all night. I already knew that Carlos III Avenue was *not* walking distance from Lawton.

I clang to Carlitos and Sandra and hollered that I wanted to stay with them. Carlitos gave me a pink bow adorned with sequins that he had probably stolen from his sister. "We'll get married someday," he said solemnly. "I will love you forever, *mi amor*."

I still refused to leave but Muñeca promised that we would return to Lawton soon. "We'll be back this weekend."

"And grandma will take me to Carlos III Avenue every Sunday," Carlitos added, hugging me.

Her Immenseness, who was still under house arrest, had made pumpkin custard especially for me.

"Here, take your Sashenka doll," Sandra said, giving me one of hers.

I couldn't stop crying. Something told me that I would never see my friends again. When I turned to *la otra*, hoping she would contradict me, I found out that she wasn't by my side anymore.

§ § §

My parents had rented a moving truck. Luisito, Muñeca's protégé, came to help and other neighbors also lent a hand. The heavy dining room set, made of mahogany and with a marble top table, raised eyebrows and complaints but it was finally loaded in the truck with the rest of the furniture. Papucho rode in it with the driver. Doctor Orozco came in his Lada, where the rest of us squeezed together carrying the smaller and more valuable items in suitcases, purses, boxes and bags.

"Goodbye, San Anastasio!" Ma mère exclaimed with a sigh of relief. "A new house means a new life."

Doctor Orozco started the car. Muñeca crossed herself, devotedly. Then she saw Barbarita, who was standing in the San Mariano corner, probably watching us, and gave the finger to her.

"Please," Ponciano said.

My grandma and I giggled. Barbarita pretended not to notice and entered the grocery store wiggling her *culón*.

"Thank God I won't have to see her tambourine ass anymore," Muñeca said. "Hopefully, we'll have better neighbors in Centro Habana."

"There are Barbaritas everywhere," Ponciano reminded her. "*Comecandelas* are all over the place."

"Shhh," my mother pointed to Orozco's huge pink ears. After all, he was a *comecandela* too.

I looked back to our old house. A pug-nosed, red-haired girl stood on the porch, waving goodbye to me.

Se fue para no volver,
Se fue sin decirme adiós.
Muy lejos de mí se fue
Matando mi ensueño de amor.

Second part
Carlos III Avenue: 9550
Chapter 1

We moved to the Carlos III Avenue apartment in 1987. By that time Ma mère's punishment period in the clothing factory was over thanks to Doctor Orozco's intercession. She was now an editor at the publishing house Gente Nueva, only a twenty-minute bus ride from our new home.

The cemetery and the restaurants where Ponciano worked as a *colero* were also relatively close. My grandfather walked to them, thus saving the five cents that the bus ride cost. Around the corner, Papucho found a bar called El Cincuentenario that served, he swore, the best doubles in Havana. Everybody was delighted with the *permuta*. Everybody except *me*. I missed Carlitos and Sandra, the jasmine tree and my old sunny backyard. I *gua*ed constantly. And I didn't even have *la otra* to argue with.

But *la permuta* had been a wise move. Centro Habana was going through a renovation process, as *Tío* Armando had predicted. Old buildings were remodeled. New shops, bookstores and cafeterias opened. We appreciated the advantages of having left "the intestine of Havana" for one of the busiest commercial zones in the city.

"*La casa de los tres kilos* is back in business!" Muñeca announced one day, all excited. *The three-cent house* was an old store at the corner of Carlos III Avenue and Belascoaín Street that had been closed since the early seventies. "Now it's called Yumurí. There are clothes, perfumes, radios and refrigerators. Even a shoe department, imagine that...I haven't seen new shoes in years."

"Lámparas Quesada is a parallel-market shop too," said my mother. "I heard they have clocks, record players, sofas and chairs. Everything is *por la libre*, without the ration card."

A red curtain of wealth had fallen over the island. Soviet TV sets, German typewriters, Chinese blouses, Bulgarian perfumes, and Vietnamese sandals appeared in the stores that belonged to the so-called parallel market. Waiting lines were shorter there and clerks more courteous than in carded shops. We didn't need coupons, though the parallel-market merchandise was quite expensive.

The government had also allowed farmers to sell part of their crops in the *Mercado Libre Campesino*. Pigs reached legal status. A building that had belonged to the Sears firm before 1959 was transformed into a modern supermarket, *Supermercado Centro*, where imported cheese, ham, sodas and cakes filled the shelves. Buses now came in fifteen-minute intervals and were less packed. New ones from Czechoslovakia and others made in Cuba, *Omnibus Girón*, replaced the beat-up Leylands. A few more taxis began to circulate, most of them Soviet Ladas.

My teachers said that by the twenty-first century the entire planet would be one big, Marxist-Leninist nation led by the Soviet Union. The evil Yankee Empire was doomed.

"What will happen to *La Yuma* if communism takes over the world?" I asked Ponciano. Since he listened every night to Radio France International and the Voice of America, I considered him an authority on political matters.

He shrugged, "Nonsense. Communism won't make it to the twenty-first century. Just look at our old Frigidaire. It is thirty years old and works like the first day, while the brand-new Russian refrigerators don't last over six months."

This was one of the few issues he and Muñeca agreed on.

I wasn't that sure, though. Symbols of the Red Block success were everywhere. We lived surrounded by Electron TV sets, Selena radios and posters of Yuri Gagarin and Valentina Tereskova. Meanwhile, the old American cars, televisions and washing machines broke down and nobody had spare parts to repair them.

The ties between Cuba and "our partners in the construction of socialism" were stronger than ever. Sturdy Soviet tourists got sunburned at Guanabo and Varadero beaches. Cuban outstanding communists and *vanguardia* workers were in turn given trips to Prague, Bucharest and Berlin. After visiting Leningrad, Doctor Orozco brought a perfume called Red Moscow for my mother, a *matrioska* set for me and a Kremlin souvenir for Muñeca who threw it in the trash at once.

A game show conducted by Yiqui Quintana offered the winners a trip to the Soviet Union with all expenses paid. Its name was *9550* because of the distance, in kilometers, between Havana and Moscow. I had a crush on Stirlitz, a Bolshevik James Bond who had infiltrated the German intelligence service during World War II. Stirlitz was the hero of *Seventeen Instants of a Spring*, a Soviet TV series. But I couldn't stomach Soviet cartoons. Bland and full of undigested of revolutionary clichés, the characters were such ridiculous goody two-shoes that I felt like kicking their asses back to reality.

A glossy Spanish version of the magazine *Sputnik* cost only three pesos. Moscow was the engine of communism, my teachers said. From their spaceships Soyuz and Saliut to the canned meat that tasted bitter but solved urgent culinary needs, anything Soviet was "wonderful," "amazing" or "truly revolutionary," according to the newspaper *Granma.*

Things were better than ever. Yet it was then when a few critics of "this" raised their questioning heads, or at least were heard of for the first time. A satirical column by Hermes Rumbado appeared every Sunday in the newspaper *Juventud Rebelde.* He mocked inept bureaucrats, phony reporters, inflated progress reports and abusive grocery-store employees.

Rumbado and Ma mère worked together. He was one of her few "cultivated" friends who got along well with Papucho, maybe because both shared a weakness for Felito II, a homemade variety of rum. Bespectacled, black-bearded and serious-looking, Rumbado didn't fit my image of a humorist but I enjoyed reading his articles and listening to his stories.

Among other mild critics of the system was the singer Virulo. He poked fun at the taxi drivers that were always "going to nowhere" when hailed by a pedestrian. He sang about the flies and cockroaches that lived a happy, fat life in restaurants and cafeterias. Rumbado and Virulo followed the golden rule so as not to get in trouble. "Play with the chain, but don't mess with the monkey." The chain meant things that were wrong with "this." The monkey was *El Comandante* himself.

As a safety measure my parents kept their distance, at first, from all our neighbors. Back in San Anastasio Street, they knew that Tony and Silvana didn't like "this," even before their failed attempt to escape. No one ignored that Barbarita and Ofelia were *comecandelas.*

However, in Carlos III Avenue we didn't have a clue of who was who. The most innocent-looking person could be an *informateur*.

The Committees for the Defense of the Revolution were supposed to receive a report about every new neighbor's revolutionary standing. But except for political prisoners and well-known dissidents, the paperwork was often skipped. As far as we knew, nobody on Carlos III Avenue was aware that the family had wanted to travel to *La Yuma*. With luck and good behavior, Ma mère said, we might be able to erase the *gusano* mark from our foreheads and records. We just needed to be discreet.

But Muñeca soon got acquainted with all the building residents. Avelina, who lived next door to us, was a nurse at the nearby Emergency hospital and possibly a *gusana*. Her son Sergio, a bookish teenager, listened at night to the Voice of America. A bingo group met quietly (bingo was prohibited) in their apartment. Its members were old women, friends of Avelina's mother. Muñeca was invited to join but refused with her usual argument, "I don't like to be associated with *viejas*."

Mauricio Beltrán, a Chilean who had fought against Pinochet and received political asylum in Cuba, lived on the third floor. He was the only one that called our street "Salvador Allende." Carlos III Avenue had been renamed in 1973 after the deposed Chilean president, but many people kept using the old name as a veiled protest against "this."

And there was Antonieta, a divorced blonde who smoked foreign cigarettes and left a strident trail of perfume on the stairs. She turned on the radio at the highest volume and played popular, modern records. Not only rumbas or boleros, but also the "ideologically deviant" rock and roll. "That music should be forbidden," Doctor Orozco said when the *Rolling Stones* thundered upstairs.

"It's offensive and vulgar and it sends the wrong message to the Cuban youth."

Papucho couldn't stand him, "Yes, and next thing you know the government will tell us which hand we have to use to clean our asses. *No jodas*!"

I sided with Papucho. However, Doctor Orozco was not an *informateur*. He despised rock but wouldn't denounce Antonieta. He also knew that Ponciano listened to the Voice of America, which *was* forbidden, and never made a comment about it. He was a *buena gente*, a good guy.

During his frequent visits Doctor Orozco complained of his domestic woes. Though divorced for five years, he still shared a house with his former wife and their two children. He couldn't move out until they found a convenient *permuta*. But his ex-wife was determined to reject all the offers, even the good ones, to keep him trapped. "I've had such bad luck," he said. He had a way of looking at Ma mère with longing, sad puppy-dog eyes that even I felt sorry for him. He still liked her, for sure. No wonder Papucho was jealous. He called Orozco *Orejón*, Big Ears, and Muñeca baptized him as *Red Sunday* because he was always organizing voluntary work sessions on said days.

Ma mère maintained Papucho had no reason to worry. "Humberto is just a friend," she repeated. "And he has done a lot for me. Without his help, I would have never been hired by Gente Nueva."

But Muñeca, the dirty-minded, whispered, "Here comes the *replacement*," every time she saw the blue Lada parked in front of the building. Was she right? Though Papucho was a taller, more handsome man, he dressed shabbily. His work clothes were always stained while Doctor Orozco's *guayaberas* and medical smocks looked immaculate. Also, Papucho hadn't stopped drinking despite his repeated promises to do so. I didn't take them seriously anymore. And Doctor Orozco possessed an aura of self-assuredness that my father lacked, particularly when he was among Ma mère's colleagues.

Ma mère had abandoned Chanel N°5 for Red Moscow and sometimes attended to voluntary work sessions in Gente Nueva. Was she falling for her ex-beau again? The mysterious feeling that adults called "love" interested me deeply. I thought I knew something about it, having been heartbroken myself. As I suspected the day we left San Anastasio Street, I never saw Carlitos again. Muñeca forgot her promise to take me back to Lawton. Carlitos's grandmother didn't bring him to our apartment. After waiting in vain for weeks, I threw the pink bow in the rose-decorated toilet and flushed it.

Chapter 2

Visiting *La Yuma* became easier, at least for old-timers, after the Cuban and the American governments relaxed travel regulations and reestablished the Havana-Miami flights. Retirees and housewives over sixty were generally given the exit permit and a visa if a relative in the United States sponsored them. But younger people still had to go through a complicated process and climb a mountain of red tape... to be denied the exit permit in the end. Luisito had solicited it, unsuccessfully, more than ten times.

A few travelers never returned. Others came back with suitcases full of *La Yuma* stuff that eclipsed even the parallel-market merchandise. Cubans exiles also returned briefly to the island. They brought clothes, photos, videos and incredible tales of what life was like in the "evil Yankee Empire." They also brought evil Yankee money to buy in the hotel stores where ordinary Cubans weren't allowed to enter. The *gusanos* (worms) mutated into dollar-winged butterflies.

Always the opportunist, Muñeca asked her sister for an invitation letter. She applied for a visitor's visa at the American Interest Section since there was no formal United Stated embassy in the island. Naturally, she got it. "I just winked at the consular officer and he gave me the visa in a heartbeat," she boasted. "I have *sandunga*!"

Ponciano was so mad that he didn't leave his room for two days after he heard the news. As for Muñeca, she talked day and night about all the fun things that she planned to do in *La Yuma*. "First, I'll go to Macy's. That has always been my favorite store. Then I'll have to check out Burdines, hope they are still around. Wait until

I come back, dressed like a *chica americana* from head to toe...I also want to see Disneyland and maybe take a short trip to New York. Of course, I'll bring you clothes, perfumes, souvenirs.... Aren't you thrilled, Longinita?"

No, I wasn't precisely *thrilled*. If my grandma decided to stay away, what was I going to do? I had already lost *la otra* and didn't want to lose Muñeca too. She tickled me, hugged everybody and was way too clingy, in Ma mère's opinion. (My mother was more detached. She'd rather read me a story than pet me.) So I was much closer to Muñeca, who prepared my *café con leche* every night and shared with me her secrets, like the Coppelia meetings with Ramoncito.

A day before Muñeca left, Papucho told her, "Ask for political asylum and then claim all of us." But I made her swear she wasn't going to stay. What if we weren't allowed to follow her afterward?

Ma mère and I accompanied Muñeca to the airport. "Don't worry," she said. "I'll return because I love my girls. You won't be able to survive without me, will you?"

I wiped a tear away. Ma mère hung her head.

"*Au revoir,* Muñeca! Come back soon!"

Muñeca was the captain of our family boat. We called her *la mandamás,* the boss, because she made all the crucial decisions...which happened to be the right ones. She had brought us from Lawton to Centro Habana. She managed the household budget. She befriended *coleros* and grocery clerks. She cooked for the family and made special dishes for me. She braided my hair before I went to school every morning. My parents came from work and found dinner ready, a fed child and everything clean and in order. Muñeca made life easy for them. But she had kept them away from me. She was the bridge between my safe, fairytale childhood land and the adult world.

That bridge was burned after her departure. With no one else around to run interference, I stepped into the surprising, contradictory planet of grown-ups. The once distant figures of Ma mère and Papucho suddenly acquired a more defined profile. I noticed, for example, that when Ma mère was among her friends she spoke calmly and rather conceitedly, pronouncing all the letters and using sophisticated four-syllable words. "You have done a *magnificent* work renovating your house," she would say to another editor. "It's *phenomenal*, dear." But when she was around Papucho's buddies (stonemasons, mechanics) her speech changed. She dropped consonants and resorted to slang. "Cool job. *Es tremendo*, you rock."

Ma mère, the chameleon, moved from white to blue collar like a reversible coat, changing manners as she changed her perfume. My father was less pliable. A quiet guy even among his own friends, he acted awkward around writers and editors who in turn didn't know what to say to him. They seemed afraid of using a term he couldn't understand.

When the three of us went together to a Gente Nueva book party, he reached for a bottle of beer before Ma mère had time to introduce him to anyone. In a couple of hours he was *borracho perdido*, drunk as a skunk, and standing, with a precarious balance, in a dark corner of the conference room. People stared at him, Ma mère looked mortified and I couldn't help but think of how different the *replacement* acted. Doctor Orozco would have never embarrassed us like that!

"Why are you married to that loser, Carmen?" a way too frank coworker asked Ma mère right in front of me.

"Because I love him," she replied, blushing. "I know he'll stop drinking one of these days."

Papucho agreed with her. Every month he swore not

to drink anymore but inevitably forgot his promise on paydays. His favorite pledge, "I'll never drink another drop of alcohol" became sort of a family joke. He didn't drink *drops* but full bottles of Coronilla rum. After guzzling three doubles in El Cincuentenario he plopped down in bed, or on the floor, and slept until the next morning. In the meantime, Ma mère lost herself in the Gente Nueva manuscripts, wearing thick eyeglasses, a wrinkled muumuu and a resigned expression.

§ § §

Ma mère started taking me to Gente Nueva on Saturdays. Having lunch later in *El Patio*, an open-air restaurant in Cathedral Square, became a routine, one that didn't involve Muñeca's presence for the first time in my life. We did a lot of eating out because Ma mère had never learned to cook. She would look inside the old Frigidaire, sigh and ask me, "How about a couple of pizzas, *chica*?"

Gente Nueva offices were in the *Palacio del Segundo Cabo*, built in 1772 and former residence of the Spanish Captains General. Its imposing colonnades and Moorish-style archways made the *Palacio* look like an enchanted castle. A castle filled, to my delight, with thousand of books. A nerd's dream come true.

Ma mère was a well-respected editor. A young novelist of the revolution, as he called himself, once offered her an electric fan and five hundred pesos if she proofread his last novel. She refused. "I'd have ended up writing it over myself," she told me. "It was a pamphlet, so full of propaganda that the first pages made me retch."

Like leaves on our old backyard, a stack of manuscripts piled over her desk. I went through many of them before they saw the public light. I enjoyed *The Adven-*

tures of Guille, a novel by Dora Alonso, and some short stories by Onelio Jorge Cardoso. But Gente Nueva books were never my favorite. Without fully understanding what propaganda meant, I realized there was something in them that "capitalist" books didn't have. The authors had intended to show how wonderful life was in Cuba, and they had tried *too* hard.

Muñeca's absence made Ponciano nervous, though he never admitted it. After she left he developed a new quirk: an irrational fear of thieves. It didn't matter that the apartment was safer than our old house. The door was closed at all times and secured with a padlock. The Committee for the Defense of the Revolution had an active network of vigilantes that patrolled the block constantly. But he kept saying that *someone* was out there, waiting to break in.

Before going to bed he would put empty bottles, a broken chair and Muñeca's broom behind the door. Once he forgot that Papucho hadn't yet returned from El Cincuentenario. We were awakened at midnight by the clatter of shattered glass. "*Carajo*!" Papucho screamed. That was the only time I heard him swear.

A year before I would have wet my bed, out of fear. But things had changed. By then I had almost forgotten Doña Lola, convinced that I had imagined her, as I did *la otra*. I had finally drawn the line between fantasy and real life, or so I thought. Ma mère said that I had an uncommonly vivid imagination. "You may grow up to be a writer, Longina. Imagine if your books happen to be published by Gente Nueva!"

"But I will not write propaganda," I replied.

I had realized, though vaguely, that there was something wrong with "this." I began to question what teachers and books said, like the Red Block's alleged superiority and the evil nature of *La Yuma*.

I didn't question everything, however. At school I had been told that spirits, saints and *orishas* were psychological leftovers of the bourgeois society. A pioneer was not supposed to take them seriously. Dialectic materialism explained all that, *Maestra* Elena assured me. I felt and slept better after accepting her views. I *gua*ed less and looked forward to taking a dialectic materialism course in secondary school. But then Doña Lola reappeared, challenging my teachers' assertion and my own sanity.

§ § §

The elementary school I attended in our new neighborhood was named Ho Chi Minh after the Vietnamese leader. It was a small, dilapidated building with faulty plumbing that had been a private house before the revolution. It had hot classrooms, warm water in the drinking fountains, cold teachers and a myopic principal nicknamed Squinty. But I preferred it to the old school since nobody there knew that my family had applied to leave the country. I didn't have to put up with a "mentor" or do extra homework on revolutionary values.

The days started with *el matutino*, the civic act. Flanked by a statue of José Martí, a Cuban flag and a Che Guevara poster, Squinty fed us every morning our daily dose of revolutionary blah-blah-blah. Students were expected to attend the civic act with washed faces, neatly pressed uniforms and crisp red berets. Until Muñeca left I was always presentable, but afterward I showed up with unmatched socks, wrinkled blouses and messy hair. It took me around a month to learn the most rudimentary grooming rules.

During the civic act a communiqué in praise of a revolutionary hero, generally dead, was read. We sang patriotic hymns and recited verses by Nicolás Guillén or another revolutionary poet. We also chanted the daily slogan. It went something like,

We are building tomorrow's society
With today's sweat, a notebook and a gun.

Or

If I move forward, follow me.
If I stop, push me.
If I back off, kill me.

At the end of the civic act we repeated: "We Pioneers want communism. We will be like Che!" and marched to the classrooms singing a revolutionary hymn or a translated Russian ballad like *Katiuska*. Posters of Marx, Lenin, Gorbachev and the ubiquitous Che Guevara watched us from the walls. Copies of *El Comandante*'s speeches, cut from the newspaper *Granma*, were placed on the bulletin board every month, or as often as he delivered them.

Only two bathrooms served the entire school. Faculty and students, males and females, used them indiscriminately. Having no toilet paper, everybody resorted to notebooks or, in emergencies, to the dusty pages of *Granma*. Teachers took care of their business in front of us. My classmate Rudy informed me that *Maestra* Sabina had only two pairs of panties, both full of holes, and that *Maestra* Elena had pockmarks in her butt. He was right.

The bathrooms walls were public glossaries of profanity. They advertised all the obscene words, *groserías*, I had ever heard of, and others I learned there. Karelia, the pioneer guide, tried to erase them on Monday mornings. A few hours later someone came and replaced them, adding more *groserías* to the already ample list.

Lunch consisted of insipid black beans or watery red beans, rice, and, when we got lucky, protein. "Protein" meant a chicken thigh, a tilapia burger or canned beef stew for special occasions like May Day. Though the food wasn't precisely of gourmet quality, I never once *gua*ed at school. My folks didn't understand that. Neither did I.

We were allowed to leave early when gas leaks occurred in the school kitchen, which happened at least twice a month. *La peste*, the stench that occupied the building like a gaseous invader, was unbearable. It was after one of these incidents that my dialectical-materialist beliefs suffered a hard blow.

It was a Thursday afternoon, a month after my grandma left. *La peste* was so strong that the principal said we didn't need to come back until the following Monday. I crossed Carlos III Avenue on a cloud of pink bliss. Little did I know that Doña Lola was waiting for me in the apartment, bellowing that old *Los Gavilanes* song, "*Oh, mi aldea...cuánto el alma se recrea al volverte a contemplar*."

She started chasing me as soon as I came in. I saw her long, dirty nails trying to scratch my eyes out...I smelled her breath, as putrid as *la peste*. And I ran away, locking myself up in my bedroom. Was she still looking for her manuscript? What did she want this time? Why didn't Ponciano help me when I called him? I still remember the episode as distorted, unconnected images from a black-and-white horror movie. An hour later, I couldn't say exactly what had happened. I only knew that it was nothing good.

Ponciano rebuffed me. "What are you talking there about Mama Lola? Cut the crap! She is in heaven now, and I haven't heard *Los Gavilanes* in more than five years." Then he added with his malevolent smirk, "*You* are crazy, girl! Be careful or you'll inherit all the family neurasthenia."

I tried to forget the incident. I attempted to erase

it from my mind as Karelia did with the *groserías* on the bathroom walls. But I couldn't. If the woman who attacked me wasn't a spirit, where had she come from? Why did Ponciano insist on denying that he had seen her too?

I didn't dare to tell my parents. They wouldn't believe me either. And I was afraid that if I mentioned the episode or even *thought* of it too much, the feared neurasthenia would get a hold of me.

§ § §

The first time I read *Coure*, by Edmund D'Amici, I thought it was science fiction. Teachers who praised their students, who smiled at them and shared their sorrows... Where had the author gotten his ideas? Not from the Ho Chi Minh Elementary School. And he hadn't been published by Gente Nueva!

We all got *cocotazos*, raps on our heads, when a teacher caught us talking, laughing or playing. *Maestra* Elena hit us with a thick metal ruler that left red marks on buttocks and backs. *Maestro* Juan also liked to beat the students, but he used his bare hands. Squinty ordered the offenders to stand in a corner for hours at a time.

No one studied for the exams. Principal and teachers wanted us to occupy a good place in an inter-school competition known as *la emulación*. After distributing the tests, they wrote the correct answers on the blackboard and walked around the classroom to make sure we had copied them. Other than that, we learned not to expect much help or indulgence. They threatened to make us stay until six o'clock and to write critical notes in our permanent records, the *expedientes*.

The *expediente escolar* contained a political, academic and social history of the student. It included a *gusano* mark if the family was or had been involved in counterrevolutionary activities. A special section was devoted to the student's political commitment. Attendance to voluntary work and Red Sundays scored high points. But Ma mère didn't allow me to participate in any of them. "God forbid you go to weed or to pick tomatoes!" she said. "I've heard that they even give machetes to kids."

Karelia scolded me. "You are too apathetic," she complained. "You don't have a good *compañera* attitude."

When I was in fifth grade, she wrote a note in my *expediente escolar* about my scarce interest in collective work. At that time Ma mère said it didn't matter. She would change her mind later, as she did about many other things.

Though they were not *Coure* characters, our teachers expected to receive frequent gifts. Teachers' Appreciation Day was one of the occasions when failure to offer at least a bottle of Fortín wine or Coronilla rum to a *maestro* could have disagreeable consequences. Gifts were always of a practical nature: a make-up kit, a blouse or a box of cigars.

My friendship with Sonia began precisely on a Teachers' Appreciation Day. Ma mère had sent two chocolate bars and a small bottle of cologne to *Maestra* Elena. Considered luxury items, chocolate bars were sold only in parallel-market stores like *Supermercado Centro*. In normal times, I wouldn't even look at them. But when I learned that they were not for me, I felt a strong, unstoppable craving. I devoured both bars before classes started.

The bittersweet taste of chocolate still lingered in my mouth when remorse overcame me. What would *Maestra* Elena say when I offered her only a cheap, made-in-Cuba cologne? I started to whimper and Sonia asked me what was wrong. She was a classmate with whom I had never spoken, a tall girl with kind eyes. "I ruined my life," I told her, dramatically. "I just ate *Maestra* Elena's present!"

Sonia shared with me her own gift, six tortoiseshell combs. But *Maestra* Elena told me the following day, "You didn't need to give Sonia half of the combs *you* got for me."

I didn't have the courage to tell her the truth, but shared all my chocolate bars with Sonia from that day on.

Eight weeks had passed since Muñeca's departure and we still didn't know when she was coming home. During a brief phone call she mentioned that, if her sister renewed her visa, she could stay up to six months.

"She may stay *forever*," Sonia warned me, "And I don't blame her. After living in *La Yuma* and eating steaks every day, who would want to come back to Cuba and black bean soup?"

I realized that my new friend didn't like "this" either.

"But Muñeca told me she would return," I said. "She can't break her promise."

"Don't be so naïve, Longina! Promises don't mean a thing to grown-ups."

I thought of Papucho and concluded that she was right.

"When adults decide to leave they do not consult us," Sonia went on. "My father left two years ago and he doesn't even pay child support anymore. He doesn't give a *carajo* if we eat or go to bed hungry."

"But Muñeca loves me! I'm her only granddaughter!"

Sonia looked at me with a sad, sympathetic expression. “That doesn’t matter, *chica*. Are you from another planet? Don’t you know that grown-ups are the weirdest beings?”

Thinking this time of my grandfather, I had to admit again that she knew more than I did.

Then I began to have nightmares. In the worst one, I received a letter from Muñeca where she announced her decision to stay in Miami. The letter ended with Doña Lola’s song, “*Oh, mi aldea...cuánto el alma se recrea al volverte a contemplar*.” Like the night *La Milagrosa* came for me in San Anastasio Street, I woke up sweating and vomiting while Ma mère tried in vain to soothe me. Fortunately, an unexpected school trip made me forget my fears and worries, for the moment at least.

Chapter 3

The camp's official name was Pioneer City José Martí but everybody called it Tarará. The kids who had been there said that it reminded them of a *La Yuma* town as portrayed in American movies from the fifties. And it made sense because Tarará was a bourgeois neighborhood of three, four and even five-bedroom villas, built just a few years before the beginning of "this."

In 1975 the entire suburb was transformed into a resort for Pioneers, after expelling or somehow convincing its original residents to move out. Elementary and middle-school students, age five to fourteen, went there as a reward if they had been outstanding communists or if their school had won the municipal competition, *la emulación*. My classmates fought for the outstanding status. Sonia, who had been in Tarará once, couldn't wait to go back. Ice cream was often included in the menu and so were chicken, ham and cheese, she informed me. All the villas were airy and clean, with working toilets.

Sonia lived with her mother and three siblings in a one-bedroom apartment. They had added a *barbacoa*, a windowless upstairs room where the three girls slept. The *barbacoa*, made of plywood, resembled a dark cage. I could hardly stand up without touching the ceiling with my head though I wasn't yet five feet tall.

I didn't qualify for an outstanding distinction. It was based on participation in political events and voluntary work. Besides, my parents preferred that I stay home for the summer, so I had no hope of visiting Tarará. "You are missing *la buena vida*, girl," Sonia pitied me.

It turned out that I would *not* miss it. That year our school won the municipal competition. All the students were sent to the camp for a whole month. Ma mère, naturally, was horrified. "You've never spent a night out of the house!" she repeated as the main argument against the Tarará visit.

"So what? All the other kids are going."

"But nights are still cold. You may get sick. Considering all the problems you have with food, you're likely to come back thinner, maybe anemic. You are already *tan flaquita*, so skinny... *Ay*!"

Despite her concerns, she didn't want me to miss four weeks of classes. I had my own, private reasons to leave home and insisted so much on going that she finally relented, "*Bueno*. But I'll visit you every weekend, hear?"

Papucho, as usual, didn't say a word. Ma mère didn't consult him either. I didn't know if he approved or not of the Tarará trip. But he made a wooden suitcase for me with my name written in golden letters.

"*Locura*! Longinita will be crying from the very first day," my grandma said when we told her over the phone. "Who is going to bring *café con leche* to her bed there?"

Muñeca didn't know that Ma mère had put an end to the nightly ritual. "I come home tired," she had told me, "You are a big girl now and can make your own *café con leche*." So every evening I boiled milk and added coffee and five spoonfuls of sugar, feeling grown-up and responsible in the process. Life was changing at home, and *I* was changing with it.

§ § §

Yuleixy, a girl who hung out with Sonia and me, said that she didn't bother to take textbooks to Tarará. "What for?" she laughed. "No one cares about classes there." *Maestro* Juan and *Maestra* Elena couldn't go. He had a broken leg and she was pregnant. Squinty planned to stay in Tarará for just three days a week. The student/teacher ratio was thirty to one, though several chaperones would accompany us.

"Longina, are you *sure* you want to go?" Ma mère asked for the tenth time. "I can help you keep up with the lessons."

"You know it isn't the same," I answered. "The teachers won't like that. They may get mad and give me low grades later."

"But most of them aren't going either!"

"I already have a bad note in my *expediente*," I reminded her. "Karelia has accused me before of not having the right attitude toward 'the collective.' Imagine if I also refuse to go to camp! She'll say that I'm not a good *compañera* and..."

"Good *compañera*, this!" Ma mère yelled, forgetting her proper demeanor.

But I didn't give up. After the second encounter with Doña Lola, I preferred to stay away from home when my parents weren't around. Ghost or no ghost, I wasn't going to risk another meeting. I was more than happy to move out of the apartment on Carlos III Avenue until Muñeca came back.

If she ever did.

The Great Adventure began on a Saturday morning. I carried my suitcase, two backpacks, and as many coats and winter clothes as if I were going to the North Pole for a year. (The fact that in late March the weather was warm enough to go swimming meant nothing to Ma mère.) Our bus had hard seats, greasy spots on the floor and small windows. It smelled of sweat, gas and the snacks—fish croquettes, fried potatoes, and bread with oil and garlic—that concerned parents, like mine, had given to their children "just in case."

We were laughing and singing revolutionary tunes like

Llegó el Comandante
y mandó a parar.
Se acabó la diversión.
(The Commander came
And ordered to stop.
No more fun.)

Why did *El Comandante* hate fun so much? These lines were pathetic! Yet they came from a popular song by Carlos Puebla played at every Communist Party event. Fidel Castro liked it.

Tarará's main entrance was festooned with flags of socialist countries and Pioneer emblems. The camp leader, a young man with a goatee, welcomed us. "*Bienvenidos, Pioneros!* Congratulations for winning *la emulación.*" He introduced himself as Enrique and said he would make sure we all had a pleasant stay in Tarará. He even took the time to escort us to our villa. While we walked through the well-paved streets of Pioneer City, the girls exchanged enthusiastic comments.

"Isn't Enrique handsome?" Marlene asked with a grin. She had just bought her first bra and bragged nonstop about it.

Aixa nodded. "So cool! He doesn't even look like a teacher."

"I wonder if he's married."

"He probably has a girlfriend."

"Well, if she isn't here..."

"You little fox!"

I wasn't yet interested in guys but the whispered remarks made me curious. What was Marlene thinking? She and Aixa looked quite "developed." They said that they were women, *mujeres*, because they had started menstruating. They wore make-up to school, plucked their eyebrows and, like *La Engañadora*, hid paper balls inside their new brassieres.

Adelfa, our chaperone, was a fifty-something and meticulous woman who insisted we all wash our hands as soon as we entered the house.

"*Mira*!" Sonia looked up, shocked. "What's that thing over there?"

It was a ceiling fan. She hadn't seen one before. I had, but only in movies and in the old *Reader's Digest* copies that Ma mère kept at home. Adelfa explained that the fan had been installed by the first villa owners, selfish bourgeois who enjoyed all the good things in life while the proletariat toiled. It was later discovered that the artifact didn't work.

"Is it out of order?" Sonia asked Adelfa.

"No, but it isn't connected to electricity."

"Why not?"

The chaperone shrugged. Maybe the idea was to protect us, proletariats-in-training, from the decadent pleasures of the defeated bourgeoisie.

The nights when movies were shown in *El Anfiteatro* turned out to be the most exciting part of our Tarará stay. Not because of the films, however. They were unpalatable World War II Soviet flicks and dull documentaries about Cuba's sugar production. But darkness gave shelter to precocious couples that later shared their experiences with the rest of us.

A clique of *chicas* led by Marlene acted like grown-up women and flaunted their obvious "development." They didn't usually mingle with the underdeveloped. We were still little girls, as far as they were concerned. But sometimes they condescended to enlighten us about the truths of life, as they put it.

Most boys, however, were still childish brats. Their opaque gaze contrasted sharply with the wild spark that danced in the *chicas*' pupils. They played baseball, wrestled, and plotted how to go to town without permission. They ignored the girls or made fun of them. "These kids are *so* immature," Marlene complained, rolling her blue-lined eyes.

Older boys were in great demand. They had managed to flunk one or two years despite the good grades that were practically forced on us. Rudy was one of them. He and Aixa were considered an established couple because they had been together for six weeks. They sneaked out as soon as the film started and hid among the palm trees that surrounded *El Anfiteatro*. Hours later, when we all were in bed, Aixa regaled us with stories about what she had done and planned to do with Rudy. Marlene encouraged her or offered advice.

"Yes, you can allow him to touch you down there, but wait a couple of days more. He has to *beg* for it."

"Uh... I already let him," Aixa admitted. "Did I do something wrong?"

"Not really. But don't take off your panties yet, okay?"

"Shut up!" Adelfa yelled when discussions became too explicit. "You are still minors. You can't talk like that!"

Aixa and Marlene laughed under their breath.

"Are you already a *señorita*?" I asked Sonia one night.

"No, thank God," she answered. "Girls feel horrid pains when they have their period. And if a *señorita* gets too close to a boy, she can get pregnant just like that," she snapped her fingers. "I'd rather wait until I'm really old, twenty or so."

"Me too," I agreed. "But I'd like to have a boyfriend, someday."

"I'll ask Esbieta how to find a good one."

Sonia's older sister, Esbieta, had no shortage of guys. Once she was even chosen Carnival star, *una estrella.* (The old titles of queen and princesses weren't socialist terms.) The floats that paraded along Malecón Drive during the 26th of July celebrations carried *estrellas* and *luceros*, pretty girls that danced in skimpy clothes. But not *too* skimpy, eh. They still had to look like decent *compañeras*.

Esbieta was proud of her gazelle-like figure, thick eyelashes and big brown eyes. She was smart, too, and had already applied to medical school. Sonia said that the only thing her conceited sister didn't like about herself was her name. Their mother had wanted to call her Svieta, after the heroine in a Soviet movie. But when Esbieta's father went to the *Registro Civil* offices to record the girl's birth, he was drunk and misspelled the name. Esbieta had sworn to change it as soon as she turned twenty-one. "She wants to be called Brooke," Sonia said, "like Brooke Shields."

Our meals were served in *El Comedor*, a spacious dining hall. We got meatballs, fish, Russian canned meat, macaroni, and cookies. Sometimes we were even allowed to have seconds and Sonia never turned them down. I enjoyed the camp's food more than Muñeca's lovingly prepared dishes. Nobody asked if I wanted more chicken or said I would starve if I didn't eat enough. Finally free from anxious gazes and *gua* fears, I devoured every bite and I didn't throw up, though I never had time to lie down after eating.

"You're filling out nicely," Rudy told me once, after looking me up and down the way guys did Muñeca.

I was ecstatic. Would it be possible that I had started "developing" too?

Yuleixy rushed out of the bathroom with a towel wrapped around her waist. She told Adelfa that a man was peeking through the window. "He was looking at *me*!" she yelped.

Nobody took her seriously.

"Who is going to waste his time watching you, scrawny bird?" the chaperone asked.

Poor Yuleixy was weighed less than a hundred pounds and didn't need a brassiere yet.

Two nights later the chaperone next-door saw a shadow near their porch, around ten P.M. She cried for Pancho, the old security guard who patrolled Tarará in a faded *miliciano* uniform. When Pancho showed up he didn't find anything out of the ordinary, but everyone felt nervous.

Then Aixa returned from a date with Rudy and noticed a presence close to our villa. "There was someone behind the bushes," she said. "He ran away before I could see his face."

"What if it was a ghost?" I asked Sonia, thinking of Doña Lola.

"If a ghost wanted to scare us he would come in instead of hanging out in the dark," she said.

Students who lived in other houses weren't bothered. But the atmosphere was charged. Even Adelfa saw "something" one evening. Soon all the Tarará residents were talking about a Peeping Tom, a *rascabucheador* that haunted the camp at night. Movies were cancelled for the rest of the week. During a civic act, Enrique, without openly acknowledging the presence of an intruder, urged us not to leave the houses after dark and to report to him any suspicious activity. He also promised that *milicianos* from the nearby town would start patrolling the camp's streets soon. "Most people here are revolutionaries," he said, "but there are still some lawless individuals around."

When parents came to visit on Sunday, two girls and a boy left. They had probably mentioned the *rascabucheador's* forays. If Ma mère found out, that would be the end of my Tarará days, too. So I kept my mouth shut. I was afraid of the Peeping Tom, but still felt safer there.

Not too safe, though. Nobody did. Yuleixy refused to go out after six P.M. Even Aixa stopped seeing Rudy in *El Anfiteatro*. Armed with a metal cane, Adelfa walked around the house before turning the lights off. She made sure that all the windows were closed and the main door locked.

"Just in case" Sonia and I started to cross ourselves at bedtime. We muttered, "In the name of the Father, the Son, and the Holy Spirit," after covering our heads with a sheet. Caution was recommendable. Praying was a bourgeois habit, like celebrating Christmas or owning ceiling fans.

Only Marlene laughed. "You are such chickens! Real men don't care for little girls. Aixa and I should be careful because we are the only pretty women here. But you—bah! You wish!"

Fortunately, after Enrique's speech the Peeping Tom vanished. No one saw any more strange shadows at night. Movies were reinstated by the third week. The local *milicianos* didn't come to patrol Tarará streets.

Rudy and Aixa resumed their dates at *El Anfiteatro*. But he dumped her, she told us sobbing, because she didn't allow him to put his little *pinga* in a certain private place.

"Why didn't you, silly?" Marlene asked. "Do you think that your *papaya* is made of glass?"

"But *Mamá* told me that my virginity..."

"Your *Mamá* isn't here! And we have no use for 'virginity' anymore. That's so old-fashioned. Let me tell you, the first time I was with a guy, he..."

"Shut up!" Adelfa yelled, "Or I'll send you back home tomorrow morning. *Qué cochinas*!"

Even Muñeca would have reddened had she heard Marlene's comments, I thought. And Ma mère! She wouldn't have allowed me to stay one more hour in the company of these "developed" girls...

§ § §

When we left the camp no one seemed to remember the *rascabucheador*. He had disappeared, just like Marlene's virginity, if we were going to believe her. I still didn't, really. I thought she was a bluff. But, on our way back to Havana, I overheard a dialogue that shed light on a few obscure points.

"Yuleixy almost spilled the beans," Marlene muttered. "He was waiting for me *that night*. Then everybody claimed that they saw 'someone' too. Monkey see, monkey do, you know."

"But he wasn't careful," Aixa replied. "I also stumbled over him once. You should have warned me."

"I wanted to, but he's a youth leader. And I am—," she chortled, "a minor, as stupid Adelfa said. I didn't want to get him in trouble."

"Are you going to meet him again?"

"He promised to call me. But I can't go to Tarará by myself and he has to stay there until August. Anyway, I don't care. I left two other guys in Centro Habana. Too bad none of them have beards."

I was shocked. Unlike Aixa, Marlene was, for sure, a *mujer*. But Enrique, what kind of a guy was he?

I had learned more during those four weeks in Tarará than in the whole semester in Havana, though not precisely about school matters. And the short period away from home also had a positive effect on my appearance. To my parents' amazement I weighed five pounds more when I came back. I even started "developing" a bit in the upper region and nursing dreams of a brassiere. My *gua* fits stopped and I continued to gain weight. Muñeca would be pleasantly surprised when she returned.

But when would she? Though Miami was only ninety miles from Havana, it sometimes seemed as far as Moscow—nine thousand five hundred and fifty kilometers away.

Chapter 4

Hamburgers bought at any cafeteria, plump pizzas from La Romanita, fried chicken from El Pío-Pío, lard-oozing *chicharrones*, condensed milk...Ah, condensed milk! I got so hooked on it that I would drink half a can daily, or a whole can if I could get away with it. Even Ma mère's concoctions tasted good. Pleased at first, she began to get concerned as I earnestly cleaned my plate and then asked for more food. "Longina, be careful or you'll end up *una cerdita*, a little pig!"

I was lucky that my appetite improved during a time of relative abundance and reopened restaurants. Ponciano's work as a *colero* turned out to be a definite advantage. Like *Celia Cruz* in Lawton, my grandfather was a professional, and clandestine, queue stander. He secured a place in a restaurant waiting line and sold his *turno*, the right to occupy a table, for forty or fifty pesos. My parents and I used the *turno* when Ponciano's clients failed to show up.

Ponciano's customers were "former members of the bourgeoisie," too proud or old to stand in line under the sun. They tried to preserve a Cuba that slipped from their fingers with every Red Sunday that passed and with each thundering speech *El Comandante* gave. Eating out was one of the cherished routines they fought to maintain. Sipping *mojitos*, they evoked the Christmas parties they had celebrated, the Plymouths and Studebakers they had owned, and the relatives and friends who from Miami also waited for the fall of "this." They still hoped for a reversal of fortunes and whispered about real or imagined conspiracies.

"There is another uprising in El Escambray Mountains."

"It doesn't matter if we have more food now, man can't live on bread alone."

"Radio Martí said that Reagan is going to send troops here."

There was a couple, *los* De Soto, that reserved a *turno* every Saturday evening. Sometimes they invited Muñeca and me to join them. Too bad that it happened when I was still *gua*ing and didn't care for food.

A senator during Prío's presidential term, *Señor* De Soto was a tall, good-looking gentleman and an operetta connoisseur. *The Merry Widow* was his favorite. "You'll find me at Maxim's," he hummed while escorting us to the table. He and my grandma were always chuckling for no reason and hugging each other, even in front of his wife. I had the hunch that he and Muñeca had once been more than friends. Ponciano disliked *Señor* De Soto, though he didn't allow that to interfere with business.

Señora De Soto wore a silvery hairnet over her white hair, pearl necklaces and a permanent, bitter grin. When asked how she was, she shrugged and answered, "Enchanted with life. How else could I be? *Encantadísima*!" and smiled with an irony that I couldn't yet understand.

All *coleros* operated illegally and had agreed to divide the territory. Ponciano got an area of the coveted El Vedado that included La Torre, El Polinesio and El Conejito. From the top floor of the Focsa Building, La Torre patrons enjoyed a panoramic view of the city. Swimming pools looked like blue eyes opened in Havana's brown face. The white plumes of steam coming from the oil refinery Ñico López wrapped the harbor in a veil. La Torre served international food but I always ordered *bistec de palomilla*, sirloin steak with onions, rice and black beans.

Lovers of Asian cuisine favored El Polinesio that had old bamboo curtains and fishing nets on the walls. Its *maripositas chinas*, tiny fritters stuffed with cheese, ham or vegetables and covered in a spicy sauce, were memorable. In M Street was El Conejito, specialized in rabbit. Copper pots hung over a fireplace. Stylish waiters, a red carpet, wood beams and oak chairs created a cozy, foreign ambience...

Old fashioned restaurants like these offered a glimpse into a pre-*Comandante* world of courtesy and wellbeing. Like the Tarará ceiling fan, they were symbols of a bygone era. I loved them. But it was precisely in La Torre where disgrace struck us, finishing the damage started by the ill-fated Christmas pig.

§ § §

Ma mère was in a bad mood. Papucho had just stopped by El Cincuentenario and gulped down a few doubles. Only two days before he had formally assured her he wouldn't "drink another drop of alcohol." Why she believed him every time was a mystery to me. How could she be so naïve? Even *I* knew he was lying.

But in the last months she had been testier than usual about his binges. They did irritate her, for the first time since I could remember. On several occasions she had compared Papucho, unfavorably, to Doctor Orozco, "I wish I had married a respectable man like Humberto and not a drunkard like you!"

"You can still marry him," Papucho mumbled.

"I may!"

Tensions mounted. My parents didn't quarrel the way some of our neighbors did, with *groserías*, fistfights and police intervention. But I felt as if we were on top of a boiling pot, waiting for it to explode.

When Ponciano called to announce that his La Torre customers hadn't arrived and we could take their place, Ma mère wasn't enthusiastic. But Papucho and I insisted. "We just have rice and eggs in the refrigerator," he said.

"And I'm hungry," I complained.

"You are *always* hungry now," she snapped.

Anyway, she caved. Before leaving the house my mother put on an evening dress and I also chose what she called "a decent outfit." But Papucho didn't bother to change his work clothes despite the quarter-sized hole that his pants had, right in his *culo*. "We're coming right back after eating, no?" he shrugged.

"But we can meet someone there," Ma mère replied. "It's Friday night!"

"Ah, forget it. Everybody is at home watching the Brazilian soap opera. Let's go."

Ma mère said nothing but curled her upper lip. I privately agreed with her. La Torre was a popular, chic spot. Why didn't Papucho make an effort to look more presentable?

As always happens when you'd rather avoid acquaintances, we met *two* of them.

"*Hola*, Carmen!" a couple waved to Ma mère from a La Torre table.

They were María Luisa, the pretty, well-groomed Gente Nueva acquisitions editor, and her husband Lizardo, an engineer. Ma mère waved back, glancing at Lizardo's dark pants and crisp white *guayabera*. Then she looked at Papucho's shabby attire and sighed.

Among the adult stuff I had recently learned was home economics. I knew that Papucho contributed modestly to the household budget. Part of his salary went to the common fund used for grocery, electricity and gas expenses. But when the time came to pay for clothes, vacations and outside meals, he had already drunk the rest of his money. It was Ma mère's responsibility to take care of all the extras and that often required complicated maneuvers. If we were in a restaurant, she would slip some money into Papucho's hand and let him pay. *Qué vergüenza*, she would whisper, embarrassed. But my father didn't look remotely ashamed and took the crumpled pesos without delay.

The waiter brought us assorted ham and cheese cuts, garnished with olives.

"Do you have any money?" Ma mère asked Papucho in a low voice.

"Me? Just ten pesos. El Cincuentenario has now parallel-market prices, you know?"

A meal for three wouldn't cost less than seventy pesos at La Torre. Ma mère sighed again, with the face of a martyr.

"Put your left hand on mine," she told Papucho. "On the *other* hand, the one under the table! I'm giving you four twenty-peso bills. Hide them in your pocket. Wait, María Luisa is watching! Pretend you are looking for cigarettes. Take them out. Not the money, the cigarettes! Put the cigarettes back now. You aren't smoking those cheap *Populares* here!"

"You bet I am!" Papucho said and lit up a *Popular* cigarette that stunk to high heaven.

I laughed and choked on an olive.

"You both love to annoy me!" Ma mère whined and looked ready to burst into tears.

Sensing trouble, I retreated to the restroom and spent a few minutes there, waiting for the smoke to clear. When I returned Papucho announced that he needed to go to the bathroom too.

"What for?" asked Ma mère with a distrustful look.

"I want to pee."

"Hold it."

"I can't. I'm going to do it right here," Papucho grinned. He started fumbling with his fly and whistling "You'll find me at Maxim's."

María Luisa, her husband and two other couples stared at us.

"Okay, okay," Ma mère said. "But come back immediately, eh!"

Papucho went away. The waiter brought three sirloin steaks buried under caramelized onions and a bowl of white rice. I attacked them at once.

"This is the longest pee in history," Ma mère said after ten minutes.

"He may be doing *caca*," I replied.

"Don't talk about *caca* at the table!"

I hadn't yet finished eating when she dragged me to the men's restroom. We only found two bearded guys who resented the intrusion. "*Compañera*! Did you lose anything here?"

Ma mère was shaking, but she managed to feign a smile when we passed near María Luisa and Lizardo.

Papucho's food was getting cold. "May I eat his steak?" I asked, ogling it.

"I don't care."

I got at it while Ma mère searched in vain the bar and the terrace. She came back livid.

"He could be smoking in the street," I said when just a couple of onion rings were left on Papucho's dish, "Because you don't like the smell of his *Populares*."

"Don't be so silly, *niña*!" she exploded. "Remember what happened with the Christmas pig? Now he's done it again. And I gave him all I had in my purse! How am I going to pay the bill?"

"Borrow some money from María Luisa," I suggested.

"Never! What is she going to think? The humiliation, *la vergüenza*!"

"Let me run home and ask Ponciano for a hundred pesos."

"You won't be able to find your way back to Carlos III Avenue. *Ay*, if only your grandma were here..."

How we missed *la mandamás* then! Ma mère and I looked at each other in despair.

"I could call Humberto...," she started saying.

"Do you know his phone number by heart?"

"Huh? No, I don't," she stammered. "We'll call your grandpa instead. He's going to get upset but I have no choice."

María Luisa and Lizardo stopped by our table on their way out. Noticing Ma mère's distress, María Luisa asked, "Are you okay, Carmen?"

"Oh, yes!" she answered with a yelp. "I'm enchanted with life. *Encantadísima*!"

Grudgingly, Ponciano came to our rescue. As we waited for him, I made a piece of chocolate cake last forty minutes while the waiter lingered around, concerned.

Papucho showed up at midnight smelling like a brewery and slept contentedly on the floor. I went to bed assuming that the incident would be forgotten soon. Hadn't Ma mère always forgiven him?

But the following day she put his scarce clothes that smelled of sweat, cement and alcohol in a brown paper bag. She collected his tools, threw them in his toolbox and said to Papucho, "I've had enough. Get lost!"

"Carmen, *mi vida*, I swear it won't happen again," he began his customary speech. "That was the last drop of..."

"You are a liar. A drunkard and a shameless liar.

This is all over. Go!"

"What has gotten into you, *chica*?"

"I can't stand you anymore. Get out of my life or I'll call the police!"

"You should have never set foot in our home!" Ponciano yelled, unexpectedly coming to my mother's help. "*Fuera*!"

With one hand he brandished Muñeca's broom as if it were a sword. In the other, he held the Paris urinal, full of pee. The scene was comical and sad at the same time, like a Soviet cartoon. But I was so scared I didn't dare to move, much less to intervene. Papucho finally left with his head down, crying and dragging his toolbox.

"He is the most impotent man I've ever seen," Ma mère declared after closing the door behind him.

"I have read that drinking damages a guy's ability to...," Ponciano said, with his malevolent smile.

"Dad, I'm talking in a metaphorical way," she replied, embarrassed. "Don't take everything literally, please!"

Au revoir, Papucho! But that couldn't be happening. Not in our family. My parents couldn't get a divorce, like Sonia's. There had to be a way of solving the problem. Maybe *I* would be able to straighten things out. I'd give it a try, at least.

"Don't you care for Papucho anymore?" I asked Ma mère. "You've always said that you loved him."

"I thought I did," she admitted. "I also hoped that he would change someday. But I realized I was wrong in both cases. I was just *sorry* for him. And he will never change. I lost count of how many times he swore he wouldn't drink another drop of alcohol. Well, what he did at La Torre was the last drop for *me*."

"But where is he going to go? He doesn't have a place to live!"

"He can stay with his mother, or move in with a friend. I don't know. And I don't care, either."

"But he..."

"Longina, stop it. You aren't old enough to understand this. Go read a book."

With that, she dismissed me. I cried until my eyes itched, like the day we had moved from San Anastasio Street. My little world was shaken every time it turned around its axis. Muñeca had gone away. My father was kicked out. In between, Doña Lola reappeared. Were we jinxed or what?

When Muñeca was home things worked differently. Better. But wouldn't she stay in Miami forever, lured by *La Yuma*'s siren song? No, she had to return. She had promised. She had said that she loved "her girls." But I was learning not to trust everything the adults said, particularly in matters pertaining to *love.*

Un jardinero de amor

Siembra una flor y se va...

We didn't go back to La Torre until several months had passed. *Señora* De Soto died of cancer that year and her husband moved to Asilo Santovenia, a Catholic nursing home. I didn't see *Señor* De Soto again, but thought of him, and of Papucho, every time I heard one of *The Merry Widow* songs.

Chapter 5

Muñeca phoned us now and then. Life in *La Yuma* had changed considerably, she complained, having taken a turn for the worse. Cecilia and her husband lived in a small bungalow in the Southwest area of Miami known as *la Sagüesera*. He drove an old Buick while Cecilia, who hadn't learned to drive, used public transportation or was chauffeured around by their children. None of them ever visited the Colony House. Instead of taking her to Macy's or Burdines, they asked her to do her shopping at the local flea market.

"I'll be ready to go back after the three-month visa expires," Muñeca whispered. "My sister had a conniption fit yesterday because I ordered two desserts at the Versailles restaurant on Calle Ocho. She's turned into a penny-pincher!"

Suddenly my grandma stopped calling. She had mentioned that it could take hours to get in contact with a Cuban operator so we didn't worry at first. But the silence continued for two weeks. Ma mère checked with *Tío* Armando, who offered her these consoling words, "If she got sick, she may die without care. Hospitals aren't free in *El Norte*, hear?"

"And Cecilia only thinks of herself," Jacinta added. "She is not going to spend *thousands* of dollars in doctors and drugs."

But *Tío* Armando and his wife were angry at Cecilia for sponsoring Muñeca. I didn't believe them.

Ma mère phoned Miami. Cecilia accepted the collect call, but informed her that they were quite expensive. "Muñeca isn't here," she said curtly. "Don't worry. She's okay. Goodbye."

"What has my mother done, *San* Millán de la Cogolla?" Ma mère cried out. "Where is she?"

A horrific thought crossed my mind. An American millionaire, like that Manhattan banker, had fallen in love with Muñeca! Didn't she exude *sandunga*? She could be in New York now. Or in San Francisco. Or in the heart of Paris, for all we knew.

Ponciano didn't say much. He kept to himself, as usual. I didn't understand why he wasn't anxious too. Or jealous. Or mad! After all, Muñeca was his wife. How could people be married and not care for each other? Or maybe he was covering up his true feelings, as my mother did, I was convinced, about Papucho.

§ § §

Life went on, though never as before. It couldn't be the same without Papucho and Muñeca. I found comfort in food—who would have ever thought it?—upgrading my condensed-milk binges to one and a half can. Sometimes I mixed it with *malta*, a bittersweet soft drink, and added a cheese sandwich. And that was just a snack. So I wasn't surprised when the scale informed me that I weighed one hundred and ten pounds. Being only five feet tall, I was in serious danger of looking like a well-fed pig. But even *la malta con leche* couldn't dilute my concern for my grandma's fate.

"Do you think she's okay?" I asked Ma mère, anxiously.

"Who knows, Longina? She could have been mugged, raped... People in imperialist societies become heartless and dangerous."

That was Doctor Orozco's style and I recognized it at once.

"Or maybe she's found a boyfriend," I replied, trying

not to sound too alarmed.

Ma mère blushed and hurried to the kitchen, saying that she had made chicken with rice that night. Then I wondered if *she* wasn't the one with a boyfriend. Doctor Orozco visited us daily and took her out on Saturdays. Hum.

§ § §

Papucho had moved in with his mother. Grandma Rosa had a room in a large, noisy tenement. I had been there a couple of times, years before, and still remembered the strong smell of fried onions that pervaded it. And the music. Salsa, rumba, conga, and merengue came from half-open doors. *Chiquichá, chiquichá.* A torrent of drums and maracas flooding the tenement, the block and the whole neighborhood...

I wanted to visit Papucho but didn't know how to get to Los Pinos, a working-class suburb in the outskirts of Habana. He had come back three times, drunk, and wept at our threshold. Ma mère had refused to let him in. "You can only come here to see *la niña*. But first you have to sober up," she warned him.

Though I still pleaded for his return, I knew it was not going to happen. He had been *replaced* for good.

Ma mère seemed much happier, and younger, since Papucho wasn't around. She started wearing contact lenses and threw the old muumuus away. When Doctor Orozco picked her up in his Lada she ran downstairs to meet him, smelling of Red Moscow and with a *quinceañera* smile on her face. She hadn't smiled like that in years.

Papucho stopped drinking, at least for a while. He came by every weekend. But his visits became less frequent after he found Doctor Orozco in shorts and sandals in our living room, as if he were in his own house. And when I told him that *Orejón* had spent the night in the apartment, he looked devastated. I cursed my big mouth. From then on Papucho would phone and ask me, "Is that man there?" before going upstairs. If I said "yes" he just waited for me in the street.

"How does 'that man' treat you?" he asked.

I had no complaints. Doctor Orozco knew that I was a bookworm. He bought me a stack of novels, favoring Russian and Soviet authors. I liked Dostoevsky's *The Gambler* and *Crime and Punishment*, but couldn't finish *How the Steel was Tempered*, by Ostrovsky or *Panfilov's Men*. Fortunately, Orozco, like Ponciano, was also an admirer of all things French and introduced me to Jean-Paul Sartre and Romain Rolland. Yet I suspected that Papucho wouldn't appreciate such details.

"Fine," I said.

"If he ever gets disrespectful, tell me right away, hear? And don't let him get too close to you."

I didn't understand what he meant until Sonia enlightened me.

"Some stepfathers get frisky with young girls," she said. "Haven't you watched any soap operas?"

"No. TV bores me."

"Well, start watching it. Soap operas are more interesting than books. And they will teach you a few things you need to know."

Papucho had no reason to worry because Orozco didn't even give me a goodnight peck. I also kept my distance. I never called him by his first name, Humberto, though at Ma mère's request I started using with him the familiar form *tú* instead of the more formal *usted*.

She hadn't told me yet about her relationship with *Orejón*. But she hinted at it by saying, "Humberto is my *special* friend. That's why we go out together and he stays here some nights. I hope it doesn't bother you."

It did and it didn't. I had mixed feelings about the whole thing. I didn't mind Orozco but wished that Ma mère had kept Papucho around, too.

Living without my father and Muñeca was hard but all families had their troubles. "Every unhappy family is unhappy in its own way," as I had read in *Anna Karenina*. Avelina, our next-door neighbor, had divorced her husband because he beat their son and got into fights in El Cincuentenario. Sonia's father had left with another woman. "Almost as young as Esbieta," she told me. "He was screwing around with her for a year until my poor *Mamá* got tired and kicked him out."

All that made Papucho look like a saint in comparison.

One day I found Ma mère sobbing when I came back from school.

"What happened to Muñeca?" I gasped.

"Nothing, nothing. It's just about your father. He doesn't want to sign the divorce papers. I could have the marriage dissolved without his signature but...," she sniffled, "I'm sorry for him."

"Would you take him back?" I looked at her pleadingly. "Just give him another chance. I bet that he has learned his lesson by now. He won't drink again, you will see."

"Do you really think so, Longina?"

She talked to me as if I were another adult. I felt responsible. I felt...*una mujer*.

"Do you think that he'll be able to control himself?" Ma mère insisted.

We both knew the answer.

"I'm going to make *café con leche*," was all I said after a long, sad pause. "Do you want some?"

"Sure."

Luisito visited us often to ask about Muñeca. At that time he worked as a janitor in the García Lorca Theater but was waiting for an opportunity to become a dancer again. He had studied ballet under Alicia Alonso's tutelage yet was refused admission to the *Ballet Nacional de Cuba* due to his "weaknesses," as his enemies put it. They called him *maricón*, a fag, and made his life miserable until he was expelled from the small ballet company he belonged to.

"Pure envy," he said once, "half of the male dancers there are as *maricones* as I am, but I just had bad luck." Then he had gone back to the university and majored in history, but wasn't able to find a job as a teacher, also because of his background.

Dancing in public and traveling to *La Yuma* were Luisito's dreams, but the former seemed easier to achieve than the latter. Older people like Muñeca received exit permits without difficulty, but young men had a much harder time. They were supposed to stay and contribute to the construction of the new society.

I felt sorry for Luisito. I already knew the stigma attached to the word *maricón* though I wasn't quite sure of what two guys would do together. Whatever it was, it had to be awfully painful, Sonia said.

One blessed Friday afternoon Muñeca called and announced that she was coming back on Sunday. I jumped up and down, hugged Ma mère and thanked all the *orishas* and saints I had heard of, including *San* Millán de la Cogolla. Good news, finally! It was about time, wasn't it?

We went to pick her up in Fernando's '55 Chevy. Orozco could have taken us to the airport, but Ma mère feared that Muñeca would say something offensive to his *comecandela* sensibilities after her prolonged stay in an imperialist environment.

Only foreigners and Cubans with passports and exit permits were allowed inside the airport building. Everyone else had to wait outside. We walked around and peeked through the glass doors that made the place look like a giant aquarium. It was called The Fishbowl.

The Miami plane arrived at four o'clock P.M., but at five-thirty Muñeca hadn't showed up yet.

"What if she changed her mind at the last minute?" I asked, trembling.

"Hush, *niña*! Don't even think about it!"

At last Muñeca appeared, hauling three huge suitcases. Her hair had been dyed blonde and cut in a pageboy style. Tall and still statuesque, nobody would have guessed that she was sixty-two years old. She could have easily passed for fifty.

"Muñeca, you've lost ten years!" I yelled, hugging her. Her Nina Ricci perfume wrapped me up like a magic *La Yuma* veil.

"And you have gained ten pounds," she replied with a proud smile. "Good for you! Carmen, you look much better too. You didn't miss me *that* much, eh?"

"We did!" I clung to her. "I hope you aren't going anywhere else any time soon."

Muñeca asked Fernando to drive through the Malecón on the way home to enjoy the sunset. The Morro Castle lighthouse winked with its only eye and the first Regla lights twinkled across the bay.

"There is no place like one's own land," my grandma said, breathing in the salty ocean breeze. "I came back because I missed you, *niñas*, but also because I found out that I couldn't be happy far from this."

"This?" I repeated, appalled. Had my grandma become a *comecandela* in Miami?

"I mean, the smell of the Caribbean," she explained. "*El* Malecón, couples by the seawall, even goofy kids in roller skates. And being able to get around on my own. Everything is so distant in Miami... If you can't drive there, you're dead. Life is much easier here."

"Yes, *la revolución* has done a lot for our country," Ma mère replied. "I guess you can only appreciate its benefits once you go away."

"Wait a moment, Carmen! Don't misunderstand me. The system is crap, and Castro is still a bearded *cabrón*. What I like is the smells, the people, the—," Muñeca paused as if looking for the right word, "The Cubanness."

A giant Cuban flag covered the façade of the Capri Hotel. Muñeca, theatrically, crossed herself as if we were passing by a church.

"But where were you?" Ma mère asked. "I called *Tía* Cecilia and she wouldn't tell me."

"I decided to live on my own...that is, to live with a guy," Muñeca answered with her usual sly smile.

"I knew you had gotten a boyfriend!" I said, elbowing Ma mère. "See? What does he look like, Muñeca? Is he American?"

"No, he's an old Cuban. And he looks just like one," she giggled, "Mustachioed, half-bald and roly-poly."

"What does he do?"

"He's a gardener. Sort of a handyman, really."

Alas for the American millionaire!

"My sister got so annoying that I'd have come home earlier if I hadn't met Felo Pérez again," Muñeca said. "Do you remember him, Carmen? He and his mother, Emilia, were our neighbors in San Anastasio Street twenty years ago. He was after me for a long time."

"Most San Anastasio Street guys were after you," Ma

mère reminded her.

Muñeca beamed, her blonde hair gliding like tinsel in the Malecón breeze.

Orozco had tactfully stayed away that night. Ponciano, after greeting Muñeca as if she had just come back from Coppelia, locked himself in his room. She didn't pay much attention to him either. Ma mère mentioned that Papucho didn't live with us anymore but didn't tell Muñeca that she was now involved with *Orejón*.

"So many things happened while I was away," was my grandma's comment. She didn't look upset about the news.

And then....parampapán.... Muñeca opened her suitcases. The living room exploded with Adidas tennis shoes, Levi's jeans, Florida Marlins T-shirts and ruffled blouses and patent-leather shoes and Hawaiian sandals and silver chains and fake pearl necklaces and plastic watches. I tried on everything. The clothes she had brought for me were a bit tight, thanks to the Tarará stay and the condensed milk consumption, but I liked that. They made me look more "developed."

She had also brought an electric fan, a blender and a blow-dryer ... A tape recorder and dozens of cassettes—ABBA, Gloria Estefan, Madonna, Juan Gabriel...A video player and a handful of new *La Yuma* movies! Plus Goya seasoning, packages of Jell-O, chicken soup cubes, bars of Palmolive soap, Miss Clairol hair dye, make-up kits, and spray deodorant.

Muñeca had made most of her purchases at *El Pulguero*, the Miami flea market where you could find anything "from a flashlight to one of these thingamajigs called computers," she informed us. Though some items weren't brand new, they smelled good. They had kept a subtle fragrance of expensive perfumes and *La Yuma* life.

When she finished unpacking, our apartment looked as if it had been visited by the exiled *Reyes Magos*. Then Ma mère and I sat around Muñeca, our ears as big as Orozco's, at least in intention.

"Tell us, tell us about this Felo guy," Ma mère urged her.

"He is a nice, decent man," my grandma said. "Generous, too. I spent the last weeks in his apartment and he asked me to stay. He even offered to hire a lawyer to do all the immigration paperwork."

I knew we had been close to losing Muñeca, but not *that* close.

"You see, he needed someone to take care of his mother. Emilia is eighty years old but doesn't want to go to a nursing home. Had I stayed, I'd have ended up as her private nurse. And I already went through that with Doña Lola, thank you very much. When my visa expired I said to Felo, 'bye-bye, darling.' And here I am. *Qué linda es Cuba, eh*!"

Chapter 6

Muñeca's return restored my lost sense of security. She got back her *mandamus* position right away, though Ma mère made a few attempts to hold on to it. I had hoped that our life would go back to normal, too, but soon I understood that I was asking for the impossible. Everything, and everyone, had changed. What would have been inconceivable a few months before had become normal now.

I didn't need Muñeca to prepare my *café con leche* at night or to help me get dressed. I ate like everybody else, maybe more than I should, and didn't *gua* afterwards. I had friends and a more interesting social life than when I was clinging to my grandma's skirts all day long. And Papucho was forever erased from our family life, though he still refused to sign the divorce papers.

"He's probably waiting for you to change your mind and take him back again," my grandma told Ma mère.

"Good luck."

"Thank God you finally got it. You put up with his drinking long enough. And you have no need to be called '*el borracho*'s wife' anymore."

Muñeca preferred "the doctor's wife," naturally. The only thing she had against Orozco was his *comecandela* standing. "The next time he tries to tell me about the great things Castro has done for Cuba, he's going to hear my opinions about the entire Politburo," she threatened.

Ponciano let it be known that he wouldn't stop listening to the Voice of America because of the newcomer. But Orozco kept his mouth deferentially shut when my grandfather turned on the radio, though he cringed every time he heard the *Yankee Doodle* tune.

He also suffered with patience Muñeca's Miami stories, stories that became wilder and more embellished as time went by. They included an imaginary visit to the Colony House and a black-tie event at the Key Biscayne Marriott Hotel. *Tía* Cecilia now lived in an eight-bedroom mansion by the sea and Felo the handyman metamorphosed into a wealthy venture capitalist, the owner of a Rolls Royce. I started to wonder if my "uncommonly vivid imagination" wasn't Muñeca's legacy. Or, simply put, if my grandma hadn't returned from *La Yuma* crazier than her mother-in-law.

Orozco was still supplying me with books. When he couldn't find more Soviet and French novels we moved on to other countries. Bulgarian author Bogomil Rainov had just been published by *Ediciones Huracán*. I read *Mr. Nobody* and *There is Nothing Better than Bad Weather* and we discussed the character of Emil Boev. But *Orejón* never got "too close" to me, physically or emotionally.

"He's careful because you are 'developing' fast and will be a *señorita* soon," Muñeca explained. "He doesn't want to get in trouble. But you have to be cautious, anyway. One never knows how men are going to react."

I hated it when my grandma talked like that. It felt as if a big, ugly cockroach had jumped out of the pages of a good novel.

Ma mère's new beau lived with us part-time. His ex-wife had never agreed to do a *permuta* and he still spent some days with his children at what he called "his other house." Though a weird situation, it wasn't uncommon at all. Sonia's father had a new woman and didn't care for his children, but kept his ration card in their apartment. That assured him a right over it.

Orozco was a true, sincere *comecandela*. Wounded at the Sierra Maestra Mountains, he still bore a four-inch scar on his neck. He kept a tarnished *Medalla al*

Valor that Raúl Castro had pinned on him in 1975. He listened devoutly to *El Comandante*'s speeches on the 26th of July, a national holiday because Castro's attack on the Moncada Garrison had taken place that day, and went to Revolution Square on the first of January, when the Rebel Army had entered Havana. He had read Marx's *Capital* and Lenin's *Complete Works*. He loved *la revolución* as much as he did my mother, but he didn't pontificate about it.

It was Ma mère, the chameleon, who adopted the *comecandela* lingo and a good *compañera* behavior that surprised everybody, including Orozco. Though we all belonged to the neighborhood Committee for the Defense of the Revolution, she had avoided participation in the night watches and skipped as many meetings as she could. But one Red-Sunday morning she proudly announced that she was going to sweep Carlos III Avenue with other members of the Committee. "We also use the street, and we are all *compañeros*," she said, hurrying downstairs with an old plastic broom.

"Listen to her!" Muñeca said, shaking her head. "Next time Castro delivers a speech, your mother will be in the first row, applauding and yelling 'Viva Fidel!'"

I finally accepted the idea that my mother and Papucho wouldn't patch things up. And I had to admit that *Orejón* made our lives easier. He would take us to Lenin Park, Guanabo or Varadero Beach in his Lada, sparing us from waiting lines and crowded buses. His patients often gave his presents (cured ham, homemade cheese, a meringue cake for Doctor's Day) that he willingly shared with us. And Ma mère showed off with him at the Gente Nueva parties where the other editors looked up to him and called him "Doctor."

Despite their political differences, Ponciano sympathized more with Orozco than he ever did with Papucho.

There were reasons. Orozco didn't like anything that came from "the evil Yankee Empire." He couldn't even stand chewing gum. Ponciano wasn't precisely an admirer of *La Yuma,* either. Muñeca's Miami adventures, past and present, real or imagined, might have had something to do with it. Like my grandfather, Orozco was a Francophile. And he was also "a professional," that is, Ma mère's equal. Both Ponciano and Muñeca agreed on that.

I finally realized that Papucho had been, all along, a stranger in our home. My grandparents had despised him. Ma mère had loved him, but that was history. And what about me?

The first time that question crossed my mind I answered indignantly. Yes, of course I loved him! He was my father! But as days passed I started to wonder how much I could have *loved* a man I didn't get to know well. Who was Papucho, really? Ponciano was defined by his French phrases and his neurasthenia; Muñeca, by boyfriends and ballads; Ma mère, by books and proper behavior. But Papucho only had his Coronilla rum bottles and he had hidden inside them.

Always quiet, even shy, my father never had a meaningful talk with me. Come to think about it, Ponciano hadn't either, excerpt during our short-lived walks in the cemetery and I had been too little then. I lived in a matriarchal society where men were like paper cutouts, more decorative than useful and replaceable any time.

§ § §

Youthful at heart at sixty-three, Muñeca was pleased with her prominent ass. It had kept tight and nicely in place, despite the passing of time. She didn't have many wrinkles or varicose veins. Thanks to her Revlon lipstick, her mouth looked pretty and pouty. She went up and down the stairs quicker than people ten years younger. And men hadn't stopped whistling at her. But her breasts had become a problem. She complained that they hung down to her knees, making her look like a wet nurse.

"It's the law of gravity, combined with the weight of life," Ma mère said. "You are no spring chicken anymore, just accept it."

"*Qué* spring chicken *ni qué carajo*? *Ay, virgen del Cobre*! My *tetas* are going to kiss the floor one of these days."

She talked freely about her beauty worries and didn't mind sharing them with me. More so since I had turned into a preteen, Muñeca consulted me about clothes, make-up issues and trend tips. "Do you think I'm too old for this, Longinita?" she asked, holding a sequined miniskirt bought in the Miami flea market.

I was no fashion guru, but I had yet to see a grandmother in a glittery miniskirt, the kind that Esbieta would wear. It would look weird, to say the least. But knowing what would please Muñeca, I didn't mind lying. "You're going to look cool in it," I said.

The next day Muñeca showed off at the grocery story in said miniskirt and a red halter top, shocking the clerks, the bystanders and the entire neighborhood.

"Pepito *el bodeguero* couldn't take his eyes off her," Avelina told us later. "He even gave her two extra ounces of coffee, so dazed he was."

Ma mère, embarrassed, asked Muñeca to dress more conservatively. But my grandma called her "old-fashioned" and went on exhibiting her risqué Miami finery all over Carlos III Avenue and the nearby streets. "Instill some good sense into my mother, I beg you, *San* Millán de la Cogolla," Ma mère pleaded to her favorite saint. "*Qué vergüenza*!" But *San* Millán didn't seem to hear her. Muñeca also donned a metallic lame dress with a low, low neckline and really short red shorts.

Now, the breast issue was more serious. After finding herself unable to squeeze into her 36-D bra, Muñeca decided that her sagging bosom needed a nip and tuck. "I want to create a *new me*," she stated. "I'm not ready to surrender yet to the law of gravity!"

Plastic surgery is free in Cuba—she had to concede that to *El Comandante*—so Muñeca quickly made an appointment at the Emergency hospital to have the reconstructive work done. Orozco laughed and Ma mère whined about the corrupting influence that Miami had had on Muñeca. As if Muñeca hadn't been pretentious all her life!

The procedure didn't take long. One morning my grandma entered the hospital carrying an oversized *La Yuma* handbag and the following afternoon she was back at home, her torso wrapped in gauze.

"Vanity of vanities, said Ecclesiastes, and all things are vanity," preached a somber Ponciano. "This woman is getting crazier by the hour."

But Esbieta rooted for my grandma. "That's how I want to be when I get old," she told me. "A bawdy broad!"

Around that time, while Muñeca waited impatiently for her new *tetas* to materialize, one day Ponciano returned from the chess club with tears in his eyes. "I don't need to go back," he announced. Ma mère sniffled. Muñeca seemed relieved. I didn't understand a thing, but by then I had given up on my grandfather. I assumed he had had an argument at the club and I soon forgot about it.

But Ponciano stopped going out from then on. He even abandoned his restaurant clients and became more of a hermit, a recluse in his smelly, cluttered room.

§ § §

Influenced by Muñeca's new-me philosophy, Esbieta, Sonia and I went to Suchel, a recently opened spa. It was the first one of its kind in Havana. Facials, highlights, perms and haircuts were done by professional stylists. It had modern steam rooms and tanned, buffed instructors who offered aerobics classes once a week.

Suchel was another instance of the changes in "this." What a few years before would have been criticized as bourgeois and superficial was now allowed and even encouraged. *Revista Opina*, a new magazine with a quite subversive title, sponsored a beauty pageant. The contestants didn't look like sweaty *vanguardia* workers. Groomed by the Suchel staff and fashionably dressed, they resembled the models in the *Vogue* and *Vanidades* magazines that Muñeca had brought from Miami.

Sonia and I couldn't afford facials. They were expensive, as Suchel followed the parallel-market policy about prices. But we both got haircuts. Esbieta's boyfriend, a young doctor, paid for her highlights.

"What do you want me to do, honey?" the stylist asked me, examining my limp and not too abundant hair.

"Whatever you want," I shrugged.

I came home looking like a distressed poodle. Ma mère said that the Suchel experience had been a waste of time and money. "Did you pay forty pesos for a crappy haircut?"

Muñeca was more encouraging. "You are a chic *chica* now," she assured me, "as you should be, being a granddaughter of mine."

A few weeks later Muñeca recovered from her surgery. She emerged from the gauze cocoon with perky breasts (a tight 34-B), a svelte silhouette, and a boosting shot of self-esteem. "I look better than ever," she bragged, posing half-naked in front of a mirror. "My *sandunga* is still intact!"

No one argued with her. The problem was that Muñeca grew fond of showing her remodeled *tetas* to everybody, including male family friends. That happened a few times, but the worst incident took place one night when Avelina and her son Sergio, a bookish college student, were visiting.

Sergio discussed with Orozco the unexpected closing of the *Mercado Libre Campesino* that had created a wave of protests. Even *Revista Opina* had run an article criticizing the move. The farmers market had solved what used to be a permanent problem in most households. Though at high prices, one could always find pork, rice and vegetables there.

"I don't think it was *El Comandante*'s idea," Orozco said. "But he's giving a speech next week. He'll explain everything."

"I hope so, and I also hope he reopens the farmers market. Nobody wants to go back to counting ration-carded beans!"

"It's not Fidel's fault. You know that the Yankees are constantly trying to suffocate our economy."

"What do the Yankees have to do with the closing of the market? Were the farmers paid by the CIA?"

"Don't joke like that! And farmers were becoming too capitalist-oriented. They thought only about making money and *El Comandante* didn't like it."

"They just wanted to be paid for their work."

In the middle of the debate, my grandma shed her blouse and called Sergio. "*Mira*, son. Don't you think they look good?" she asked, pointing to her violet nipples.

Orozco rolled his eyes.

"Uh—yes—very good, *señora*," Sergio stammered, blushing.

Ma mère, horrified, ran away to the kitchen. I adored my grandma but I had to agree with Ponciano this time. Yes, Muñeca was getting crazier. . . by the minute. What had gotten into her after coming back from *La Yuma*?

Chapter 7

Muñeca's antics didn't stop at these incidents of exhibitionism. Her artificially-enhanced *tetas* had gone straight to her head, Orozco said, and caused a short circuit there. The breast surgery was followed by a dating frenzy. For two months Muñeca went out with several guys, all of them at least ten years younger. She would leave in the evening and return around midnight, or didn't return until the next morning. And she didn't use any Coppelia excuses this time.

That went on until she met Eduardo Robles, a forty-five year old X-ray technician who worked at the Emergency Hospital, right on the corner of Carlos III Avenue and Espada Street. Muñeca hooked up with him thanks to Avelina, who was a nurse in the same place. "They hit it off at once," Avelina said. "It was love at first sight. Oh, May-December romances are so cute..."

Ma mère snorted. "*Qué* cute, *chica*? Embarrassing, that's what it is."

Muñeca spent two or three nights a week with Eduardo. But she didn't intend to live with him or, God forbid, marry him. She just wanted to have fun in a no-strings-attached relationship. "Outside Cuba, this is called women's lib," she said to me, winking. "The world is changing fast."

"Yes, life is changing in other countries," Sonia agreed. "It will in Cuba, too."

But I don't think they had exactly the same changes in mind.

Outside Cuba, the biggest shift seemed to be caused by perestroika which at first I believed was a Russian girl's name. And even later, I still had a hard time understanding it. For Orozco, perestroika was “a betrayal of Lenin’s legacy.” Ponciano, who regarded Gorbachev as a messiah, contended that it would eventually mean the fall of communism in Europe and the end of “this” in Cuba. My teachers refused to discuss it. “Let’s wait until *El Comandante* explains everything,” was all they said, nervously, when a student brought up the topic.

Though *El Comandante* took his time to offer explanations, perestroika’s effects became apparent soon. Russian canned meat disappeared from the stores. We stopped singing *Katiuska* at the school civic acts. The principal retrieved Gorbachev’s portrait from the hall. “Soviet” didn’t mean “amazing” anymore, at least according to the newspaper *Granma*. The Spanish version of *Sputnik* magazine vanished from the stands after an article in praise of perestroika appeared in it. The last issue was printed with typos, paragraphs that lacked periods and blurred pictures.

People whispered that the Soviet Union was going to be divided, East and West Germany unified, the red map reorganized. Wasn’t communism supposed to take over the world by the 21st century? What was going on with our “partners in the construction of socialism”?

I asked myself these questions because it wasn’t a good idea to ask them aloud. But I didn’t feel *too* surprised. I had always suspected that there was something wrong with “this.”

§ § §

Papucho had stopped begging my mother to take him back. He signed the divorce papers. He didn’t drink anymore, or at least he didn’t drink the days he came to see me. But he was still rail thin. His face was craggy and he looked like a much older man. When I asked him why he had lost so much weight, he said he couldn't buy enough food. Then he recited an old verse that was becoming popular again,

Si quieres comer jamón y saborear mantequilla,
Tírate al Malecón y nada noventa millas.

The circles around his eyes grew darker. The constant rumba-and-conga current that engulfed Grandma Rosa's room didn't allow him to sleep well, he explained. "That Los Pinos tenement isn't a peaceful place."

At home things weren't peaceful either. My grandparents quarreled all the time. Ponciano called Muñeca a variety of names among which "whore" was the mildest one. She seldom cooked for him, or for anybody else. She became a regular Suchel client, joined an aerobics class and began working out in the Carlos III Avenue Park three days a week.

Eduardo wasn't welcome in the apartment. Muñeca brought him sandwiches to the Emergency Hospital and took him out to the nearby Las Avenidas restaurant. "Where all the neighbors can see them," Ma mère said. "*Qué vergüenza*! Why don't they go to Coppelia or to *el* Malecón?"

One day Muñeca warned her that if Eduardo wasn't allowed to visit, she would resort to another *permuta*. She would exchange our apartment for two smaller places in order to have her own house.

"Over my dead body!" Ma mère replied. "Where are we going to move, into a one-bedroom hovel?"

"I only have one life to live," Muñeca answered with a soap opera heroine's attitude. "I don't care where I spend the rest of it, as long as I'm with the man of my dreams."

Ma mère curled her upper lip. I didn't know what to think. Was our little world going to be divided, our private map reorganized too?

Ponciano took to crying every night. He once reminded Muñeca they were still legally married. She laughed aloud. "When was the last time you acted like a real husband?" she asked. "I haven't seen the color of your...thighs in seventeen years! *No jodas*!"

He sobbed like a child and threatened to kill himself. Ma mère hurried to console him. Even Orozco said that night that perestroika might not be a bad move after all. I tried to think of something nice to say, but couldn't. Ponciano hadn't been a real grandfather either. In ordinary times he paid no attention to me. And he had played a role during my last encounter with Doña Lola that wasn't precisely on my favor.

Ma mère accused Muñeca of wounding Ponciano's feelings. "She shouldn't be parading around with Eduardo, dressed like a retired prostitute. Dad allowed her to do as she pleased and never stopped calling her 'his wife,' despite her improper behavior. Why is she humiliating him publicly?"

Tío Armando and *Tía* Jacinta said that they would disown Muñeca if she didn't mend her ways. The neighbors began to call her "Pants on fire." Even Avelina made fun of her the day my grandma showed up in the hospital lobby in a flashy, tight red dress at ten A.M.

Yes, Muñeca was taking her new-me strategy to extremes, but I didn't understand why everybody got so mad at her. Particularly Ma mère! Her affair with Orozco had started when she and Papucho were still married but no one had made a fuss about that. My family's attitude and Gorbachev's perestroika were equally baffling. Words had lost their original meaning, paragraphs without punctuation, chaotic maps. . .

§ § §

Ponciano began to die when the first summer heat

wave fell on Havana like a pillow of fire. Doctors said it was cancer. Ma mère swore it was heartbreak. At first, he simply wouldn't eat. He rejected Muñeca's meals when she, out of pity, cooked something for him. It became Ma mère's task to bring a bowl of soup to his room when she returned from Gente Nueva. Most nights she took the soup back to the kitchen, untouched.

"*You* are starving him to death," she would hiss to Muñeca. "This is your fault, hear?"

Ponciano insisted he wasn't hungry. "Old people eat less," he said when Ma mère nagged him. "Don't worry. I'm fine."

Sometimes Muñeca made a concoction of egg yolk, milk, vanilla extract and sugar, mixing the ingredients in the Osterizer. I told Ponciano that I had prepared it myself, the only way he agreed to drink a few sips.

But when he dropped to one hundred sixty pounds (he had been one hundred ninety most of his life) Ma mère panicked. She and Orozco dragged him to the Emergency Hospital, though they made sure he didn't end up as Eduardo's patient. After a quick check-up, Ponciano was admitted. He had metastasized colon cancer and pneumonia, doctors said, and wouldn't last over two months.

Ma mère, devastated, sent me home for a portable radio, a toothbrush and his beloved Paris urinal. Fortunately, the hospital was right across the street. "*Mira*, you can see your room's balcony from the bed," I pointed out when I brought his stuff.

For the first time since our visits to the cemetery Ponciano had a gesture of affection toward me. He held my hand and smiled weakly.

My grandfather stayed in the hospital for fourteen days. Muñeca went to see him once but he dismissed her. "Tell that old woman to leave," he asked the nurse. "What is she doing here? I don't know her."

The cancer, doctors said, had started in the colon and spread to the liver and perhaps to the brain, which could explain Ponciano's failure to recognize my grandma. But how come he recognized everybody else?

"He didn't want to touch me after your mother was born," Muñeca told me. "'*No me molestes*,' he would say. 'Don't bother me.' And now he acts as if I were killing him. How ridiculous!"

"She *is* killing him," Ma mère insisted. "She didn't need to shame him, boasting of her 'young conquest.' Fu!"

In the middle of the crossfire I agreed with both parties in private and tried to forget about them when they weren't around.

I didn't even tell Sonia. Though her father had left with a young woman, that happened all the time. There was a Van Van song, *La Titimanía*, about middle-aged men who left their aging wives for younger, prettier girls, *las titis*. But I had no way of explaining why my grandma was involved with a guy who could easily be her son. Women were not supposed to be titimaniacs.

It was the hottest summer that Havana had suffered in years. "It's raining fire," people complained. "*Llueve candela*." *La candela* was everywhere. It dried out the Carlos III Avenue trees, made tempers boil and burned slowly in my grandfather's sunken eyes.

As July moved into August, perestroika grew stronger in Europe. And Ponciano grew weaker in the hospital bed. I understood the meaning of the phrase "prolong the inevitable" for the first time.

Doctors sent my grandfather home. For two weeks

they had kept him fed through an IV tube. Back in his room, he refused to eat again. Orozco explained that enlargement of the liver produced an artificial feeling of satiation in cancer patients. That comforted Muñeca. Cancer, not her, was starving Ponciano to death.

Ponciano had given Ma mère power of attorney to get his pension and deposit the funds in his bank account. But he insisted on having the checkbook back. "See how he is?" Muñeca asked. "On his deathbed and still concerned about money...As if he could take it to the grave with him!"

He also wrote a private testament leaving everything he had in the bank to my mother. Orozco and Avelina signed it as witnesses. "Take the funds out immediately," Ponciano ordered Ma mère. "Before burying me, if you can. Don't take any chances, hear?"

Nobody came to visit during my grandfather's final days. His former restaurant clients had already died, left the country, or become too old. Others had lost contact with him. Since I was on vacation, Ma mère asked me to watch him and make sure he had water, soup or anything he wanted.

His room, still full of boxes and empty bottles, didn't smell of urine anymore. There was a new scent, a mix of Gravinol pills, cough syrup and a pungent odor that I feared was the smell of death.

Ponciano slept most of the time, his mouth open and his eyes closed. His breathing sounded like the engine of a '52 Ford. The first days he asked me to turn the radio on to the Voice of America so he could keep up with the advances of perestroika. But after a while he lost interest and just wanted to snooze.

Muñeca would tiptoe to his room. He was now too weak to shoo her off. She sneaked in to rearrange the bedclothes, open the balcony door or bring a glass of milk that he refused.

"Leave him alone," Ma mère said.

But Muñeca persisted. Sometimes she called him softly, "Poncianito..."

One day I heard them whisper. The next one she sat on the edge of Ponciano's bed. By that evening, she was holding his hand as he painstakingly drank a sip of her egg-and-vanilla concoction.

Later Muñcca knelt in front of Ma mère's Virgin of Charity altar and lit a candle. Was she praying for Ponciano's recovery? She never said but I knew they had patched things up. I also knew that they had loved each other in a peculiar, painful and neurasthenic way.

Ponciano died one afternoon while Ma mère was at work. I went to check on him and noticed that his eyes were wide open, but unnaturally turned upwards. He didn't react when I called him. A deep whistling came from his chest and his lips moved slightly.

Muñeca yelled for Avelina. She came, looked at Ponciano and shook her head.

"Go to your room," Muñeca told me.

"But he isn't dead," I said. "What's going on?"

"He isn't coming back, *niña*."

Muñeca crossed herself. She approached Ponciano and made the sign of the cross over him too. Then she kissed his forehead.

"Mama Lola," he mumbled.

I stayed there until the rumbling sound that came from my grandfather's chest stopped and his lower jaw dropped.

"He's gone," Avelina said.

I ran to my room. It took me a while to start crying but once I did, I thought I would never stop. I cried for Ponciano, for our walks in the cemetery, for Carlitos and

Sandra and for Papucho. I mourned the loss of a way of life that, though imperfect and crazy at times, was the only one I knew. The one I had grown up with and that was now gone, like my grandfather, without having even said good bye...

§ § §

Following Ponciano's wishes, Ma mère hurried to claim the funds he had in the bank. But she received a disagreeable surprise. All the money belonged to Muñeca because it was considered common property. Private testaments weren't valid under the revolutionary laws.

She came back fuming and told Orozco, "She's going to spend everything with Eduardo! That's all he wants from her and now he's going to get it."

Muñeca overheard the remark.

"At least he isn't a drunk!" she yelled. "And he is good-looking. You are just envious. Sour grapes!"

La candela took over. Insults and *groserías* flew back and forth, filling the apartment like poisonous gas. Orozco was forced to intervene. I felt that something precious and perishable like life itself had been broken at home.

Ponciano was buried in our family mausoleum, under the angel that spread its marble wings over the deceased Querejetas. I accompanied Ma mère to the cemetery. We were the only ones there. She didn't allow Muñeca to go and Orozco had to do voluntary work that day. *Tío* Armando and *Tía* Jacinta also excused themselves with their *comecandela* activities.

The service was brief. Ma mère read an excerpt from *el Kempis* and said a Hail Mary for the repose of Ponciano's soul. There was no mass because he hadn't been a Catholic, at least in the conventional sense. The only flowers on his coffin were five withered daisies bought at the last minute from a clandestine vendor. A hot wind blew, making my eyes itch. *Au revoir*, Ponciano!

A layer of dead leaves, dirt and grass covered the mausoleum. "This place looks so neglected," Ma mère murmured. "We'll have to get somebody to clean it up."

I noticed an inscription on the grubby tombstone—*Dolores Fontán (1900-1988)*—and pushed the leaves away to make sure that I wasn't misreading the last date. If it was right, then the day I had seen Doña Lola in our old house she was still alive. And also the second time, when we met in the apartment!

"So Doña Lola died a year ago," I said as casually as I could.

"Ah...yes," Ma mère gave a tip to the undertakers and took my hand. "Around a year ago. Let's go."

We started walking toward the exit.

"But you all said she had died before I was born!" I blurted out. "Where was she?"

"We had to intern her in the Mazorra Psychiatric Hospital," Ma mère said after a long pause, "because she once tried to kill you."

"She tried to what?!"

"To smother you, with a pillow. She sneaked into your room and...*ay, San* Millán de la Cogolla! We caught her just in time. But you can't remember it. You were only a year old and we took her away immediately."

"She never stayed with us again?"

"Only for a few days, back when we lived in Lawton. There was a hurricane and many of the Mazorra patients were sent home."

"Was it the only time?"

We passed by Amelia's grave, still surrounded by

fruits, flowers and candles. Ma mère put an arm around my shoulders and we sat on the bench where Ponciano used to rest and read. "Why are you asking me that now?"

"Because I met her twice," I answered. "In Lawton, she just touched my face and said something about her manuscript. But the second time she got nasty. She went after me, trying to scratch my eyes out. Ponciano was around," I started to shake. The memories filled me with the same anguish I had felt on that day. "He didn't even try to stop her, just laughed. He-he-he... I think he *wanted* her to get me. I hid in my room and locked the door. When I came out later, he said I had invented everything, that he had seen nobody. He told me *I* was the neurasthenic one."

Ma mère hugged me. "You should have told me, *niña*. Why didn't you?"

"I thought you weren't going to believe me either."

"Of course I'd have believed you. Your grandfather was sick. Just like his mother, though he wasn't so aggressive. It was the neurasthenia, you know? Doctors said they were wired all wrong."

Wired all wrong. That was a good way to put it. "But why was Doña Lola there that day if you kept her in Mazorra?"

"She began to have seizures. Dad brought her home so she could be seen at the Emergency Hospital. He was supposed to take her back to Mazorra before you came from school. He never told me about that incident," she sighed. "For him, his mother could do no wrong."

"He loved her a lot, didn't he?"

"More than he did Muñeca or even me."

"Did he ever visit her?"

"Yes. Oh, yes, almost daily. When we said he was going to the Capablanca Chess Club he was really in

Mazorra, with her."

"And you, did you also go to see her?"

"A few times, but she didn't recognize me."

The accumulated tension began to dissolve.

"Well, you guys created a good story," I said finally. "Better than the ones published by Gente Nueva."

"Maybe you will write it someday."

"Someday. . . "

"We all have a writer inside us. And also a neurasthenic."

"Why did you lie to me?"

"Because you were such a nervous, impressionable child... Remember how you cried at night, vomited, had an imaginary friend and played those weird games? We were just trying to protect you. I'm so sorry. I could never imagine that she..."

"That's okay. But what about that manuscript?"

"Which manuscript, *niña*?"

"The poetry book, the one she wrote."

"Well...I don't know. It must still be among my father's papers, unless he threw it away. If you want, we'll try to find it."

"Someday," I repeated.

Arm in arm we left the cemetery that had been my first playground. The white mausoleum where we had buried, at the same time, my grandfather's body and Doña Lola's ghost...

That night Ma mère turned on the radio to the Voice of America as a posthumous tribute to her father. The most important news was that Lithuania had declared its independence from Moscow. It had something to do with perestroika, I suspected. But none of us imagined the impact that the disintegration of the Soviet Union would have on Cuba, though we were 9550 kilometers away from it.

Third Part

La Lenin: Repentance
Chapter 1

The first time I heard about the "special period" was during one of *El Comandante*'s speeches, in July 1990. But there had been changes all along, subtle and not-so-subtle hints that our years of relative abundance were coming to an end.

The Communist Party had accused farmers of making too much money and of becoming "the new bourgeoisie." *El Comandante* had slammed them in *Granma* and ordered to shut down the farmers market. *Centro* was also closed and turned into a computer lab, but only those who had a special authorization could use it. Sonia tried to get one but gave up after several failed attempts. "This is worse than getting exit permits," she said, exasperated.

The "special period" crashed hard against the dinner table. Steaks metamorphosed into soy burgers. Fresh milk was only available, through the ration card, to children under seven years old. Everyone else got a dust-tasting cereal called *cerelac*. People waited in line every morning to get one muffin at the *panadería*. Grocery stores shelves were empty and so were our cupboards.

I often wished to go back to the old days when I was never hungry. Unfortunately, my appetite and my "development" increased at the same rate that food vanished. I found myself savoring as delicacies the once spurned *papitas fritas*.

Nitza Villapol recommended ludicrous recipes like meatless hash made with orange peels and mayonnaise without eggs. In the meantime, *El Comandante* exhorted us to keep the faith in communism. A song by Carlos Varela, a singer who dressed in black and at times seemed dangerously critical of "this," became the "special period" anthem: *La política no cabe en la azucarera.* (Politics can't be stuffed inside the sugar bowl.)

Many restaurants closed or, like El Portal, La Torre and El Polinesio, catered only to tourists. They became part of a separate economy, the dollar-zone businesses, where Cubans were not welcome. The Soviet TV sets, the German typewriters, the Chinese blouses, the Bulgarian perfumes, and the Vietnamese sandals left without saying goodbye. Even Red Moscow went away. It was so difficult to find new clothes that I asked Sonia's mother, a seamstress, to alter some of Muñeca's old *Yuma* dresses in order to wear them.

Yumurí, Lámparas Quesada and other parallel-market stores turned into dollar-zone shops where Cubans couldn't enter unless accompanied by a foreigner. People called the new stores "shoppings" because their plastic bags had the words "Easy Shopping" written on them. The stores' slogan was ironic: shopping there was everything but easy. Armed security guards stood by the doors and questioned the natives who attempted to come in. A foreigner had to show his passport and was allowed to bring only two Cubans with him. Nationals had become second-class citizens, as Mercedes, my first grade teacher, had said that would happen when we moved to *La Yuma*. It turned out that we didn't need to leave our country, after all.

Our neighbor Mauricio, the Chilean refugee, started a clandestine trade. He escorted those who bought dollars on the black market to the "shoppings." He showed his passport and acted as if the money were his, charging his clients fifteen percent of the amount spent.

Blackouts returned with a vengeance. The programmed ones were announced in the newspaper *Granma* and lasted for five hours, usually from seven P.M. to midnight. The un-programmed ones happened anytime and could last a whole day. Long, poorly ventilated vehicles known as camels replaced regular buses. Touristaxis and panataxis, the new yellow cabs used by foreigners, dashed through the desolate streets like flying stars.

Suchel, that modern beauty parlor, didn't accept Cuban pesos anymore. Lenin Park suffered the same fate and became a forbidden paradise. Like everything good, it was "just for tourists." They were the only ones who had dollars to eat in Las Ruinas and to arrive there in panataxis.

Frustrated Cubans left the country, legally or not, even those who had supported the revolution in earlier years. Our neighbor Antonieta and her boyfriend built a raft and fled during the May Day celebrations. They arrived in Miami two weeks later, sunburned and dehydrated. *Tío* Armando and *Tía* Jacinta, who had applied for *el Bombo*, an American visa lottery, won two visas and left in secret. We found out about it from a postcard they sent to Muñeca. "Seeing is believing," my grandma said, in shock, looking at the *La Yuma* stamp.

An old phrase from the sixties, "the good thing about 'this' is how bad it is getting," began to circulate again. But how much worse could it get? Though not too loud yet, people complained about the situation and blamed *El Comandante*. They avoided using his name, calling him You-know-who instead.

And You-know-who talked constantly about an

imminent American invasion. Murals, billboards and newspaper articles repeated and magnified his words. The Committees for the Defense of the Revolution held urgent meetings to instruct neighbors on how to act when the first *Yuma* bomb hit the city. As soon as *la guerra de todo el pueblo* (the people's war) began, older women and children would abandon their homes and take refuge in the underground shelters that were going to be built in record time by volunteer workers. Everyone else was a considered a soldier. Soldiers would go directly to control points and join their platoons. Ma mère's platoon was led by Sarita, the president of our local Committee for the Defense of the Revolution, who had never fired a shot. Orozco commanded his, which consisted of bureaucrats and white-haired retirees.

Outside the dollar zones, the entire city had fallen into utter disrepair. *La guerra de todo el pueblo* became the butt of endless jokes. "An American fighter finally comes to bomb us," Sonia told me. "But when the pilot looks down at La Habana Vieja, he believes that someone has already done the job and goes back to *La Yuma*. To celebrate our great victory against Yankee imperialism, You-know-who gives each Cuban soldier two rice sacks, one to wear as pants and one to wear as a shirt."

Despite the jokes there was a bitter mood in the streets. Rumbado's satirical column disappeared from *Juventud Rebelde*. Virulo's concerts were cancelled. *Revista Opina* stopped circulating. Both the chain and the monkey were equally dangerous and not to be toyed with.

The "special period" became a household phrase, as familiar as the long lines to buy a bag with three chicken thighs or the blackouts that lasted for several hours.

School lunches were so trimmed down that we had to bring our own meals from home. I started to find *cerelac* yummy. When mixed with three spoonfuls of sugar and enough water, it became sort of a malt shake.

And yet, life went on. Papucho found a new partner, a schoolteacher who moved in with him and Grandma Rosa. Flor was a stable person, he told me, unlike "someone we knew." He seemed to drink less now, and Muñeca joked that Flor kept him in a short leash. "Good for her," Ma mère said.

I wondered if she didn't feel jealous. Didn't she care for Papucho anymore, at all? I didn't understand how two people could have lived together, had a child, and then split up just like that. *Prácata*! But I did notice that Orozco looked nervous when Papucho came to see me. He wouldn't leave him and Ma mère alone, even canceling voluntary work when my father was scheduled to visit.

Ma mère and Orozco married in April 1991. After going to a notary public, they shared a small meringue cake, *cerelac* tartlets and three bottles of Vino Fortín at home with a few friends. Later they spent a weekend at the Capri Hotel, a privilege now reserved for foreign tourists and Cuban newlyweds. After that, Orozco began to spend more time in our apartment, though he kept his ration card in his ex wife's home.

But because of the "special period" restrictions Orozco couldn't find gasoline for his Lada anymore. He resorted to a heavy Chinese bicycle. Daily rides from Centro Habana to Lawton (he was still working at the San Anastasio polyclinic) made my stepfather lose ten pounds during the first three months. His buddies put the blame on the marriage and asked what his new wife was doing to him. But the poor guy wasn't in the mood for jokes. He started listening to foreign stations like BBC and *Radio Exterior de España*. "I am stunned," he said often. "I don't know what's going on."

No one did. Not even my teachers, or the school principal. Or You-know-who himself, whose speeches had shortened considerably. Our main partner in the construction of socialism had been dismembered. The Berlin Wall had fallen. Everybody had heard something about glasnost and perestroika but these were dangerous terms. As dangerous as the American dollars, so ideologically deviant that Cubans went to jail if they were caught with only one Yankee Empire bill in their pockets.

Muñeca also lost weight. After Ponciano's death she didn't seem happier or more liberated. Just the opposite: she talked less and was somber for weeks. And then the "special period" took its toll on her. When the last bottle of Miss Clairol was gone, gray strands replaced her once blonde tresses. She had already used all the American make-up kits, and facial powder and lipstick were difficult to find in pesos. She was getting old— fast.

Her affair with Eduardo had frequent ups and downs, and there were more downs than ups. Many Saturday evenings she wore her best *La Yuma* dress and spent half an hour reconstructing her thinning eyebrows with a brush and a tiny brown pencil. But Eduardo didn't show up. Or he came by so late that she didn't feel like going anywhere.

One day Ma mère found out that some things Muñeca had brought from Miami (a pair of low-cut jeans she never dared to wear, an iron and the blow-dryer) were missing. My grandma admitted she had sold them.

"At least, you could have told me about the blow-dryer," Ma mère said reprovingly.

"I didn't think you'd want it, and I needed the money," Muñeca replied.

"Dad had fifteen thousand pesos in his account! Did you spend all of it?"

"There are still four thousand, but I'm saving them for an emergency."

"You've been giving money to Eduardo."

"Well, I—I contribute with something. You don't allow Eduardo to come here. Fine. But he lives with his parents and two sisters. So we have to go to a *posada* every time and that gets expensive."

Posadas were cheap motels where couples went to have sex, paying their stay by the hour. They were the only places available to Cubans after hotels became dollar-zone businesses. I pretended to be absorbed in a book when Ma mère glanced at me.

"You belong in a senior club, not a *posada*," she whispered.

"Don't tell me where I don't belong!"

"But don't you see, mother, that Eduardo is just using you? For God's sake, he's twenty years your junior!"

"Didn't you pay for Papucho's dinner when you went to a restaurant?"

"Papucho was my husband and Eduardo is a vulgar gigolo. The minute you stop...contributing, as you say, he'll dump you. Wake up!"

Muñeca walked out of the room, looking hurt. I felt sorry for her. But I was also upset. I had outgrown all my clothes, including the *La Yuma* outfits. I was planning to have the bluejeans altered so as to wear them myself.

After that incident Muñeca stopped seeing her beau for two weeks. Ma mère, relieved, encouraged her to join a seniors reading club that met once a week at the Centro Habana *Casa de los Abuelos*.

"*Abuelos ni un carajo*!" my grandma huffed. "I am not *that* old yet! And I am not a library mouse like you."

Then Eduardo showed up again and Muñeca welcomed him back. Their roller-coaster joke of a relationship went on.

"Don't worry, Carmencita," Orozco told Ma mère. "Her four thousand pesos won't last long."

"I know," she answered with a sour smile. "But they were mine, too."

One evening my grandma donned a pink dress that barely covered her knees and sprinkled her neck and breasts with L'Air du Temps, a small bottle she reserved for special occasions.

"Eduardo invited me to a nightclub," she announced. "We'll go to a *posada* later. *He* is going to pay for it, by the way. Don't expect me to come home tonight."

And out she went, moving her sagging behind as fast and furiously as she could.

"How long will it take her to realize that she *is* an old woman?" Ma mère asked, sighing.

It wasn't midnight yet when my grandma came back, still smelling faintly of L'Air du Temps. She got into bed without turning the lights on and began to weep in the dark.

§ § §

A couple of days later Muñeca and I were in the kitchen boiling milk to prepare *arroz con leche*. She had bought half a gallon on the black market for thirty pesos. The phone rang and she hurried to answer. (She always did, because Eduardo hung up when anyone else answered.) I pricked up my ears, but only heard whispers and an occasional *carajo*. In the meantime, milk spilled over and trickled to the floor.

Muñeca returned and kicked a chair before sitting down. I thought she was angry about the spilled milk. "Sorry," I said, cleaning the mess the best I could. "But we can still make a little *arroz con leche*."

"What a jerk!" she sniffled. "The *cochino*, the dirty pig! Why did I waste my precious time with him?"

"Was it Eduardo?" I asked.

"It was Avelina. She told me that Eduardo has a young girlfriend. That everybody in the Emergency Hospital is laughing at me. And that he calls me *la vieja esa* and—wishes I die soon so he can inherit the little I have left."

"How can he inherit anything? You *aren't* married."

After the strife that followed Ponciano's death I had become quite familiar with legal rights.

"Shh, *niña*. Don't talk about this with anyone, particularly your mother."

"I don't gossip, Muñeca. You know that. But tell me—"

"I made a testament leaving all my money to him. *Ay*, the stupid things one does when one gets old!"

She wiped her eyes on a dishtowel, leaving a trace of homemade mascara. I looked at my grandma and saw for the first time a wrinkled woman, her face covered with age spots, her hair scarce and gray. It hurt me to realize that she was a *viejita*, an old lady like those she had always despised.

A few days later Muñeca went to a notary public and redid her last will, naming Ma mère as her beneficiary. She exchanged two thousand pesos for fifty dollars on the black market. Then she asked Mauricio to buy a pair of jeans for me and another blow-dryer. The Chilean, magnanimously, charged her only ten dollars for his services. And she didn't mention Eduardo's name again.

Chapter 2

El Comandante proclaimed with great fanfare that the 11th Pan-American Games would be held in Havana in August 1991. The new slogan, *Vivan los Juegos Panamericanos*, replaced *la guerra de todo el pueblo* and toned down the apocalyptic talks. The city went through a fast, façades-only renovation. The frequency of blackouts diminished.

Our summer vacation had already started but we sixth-graders were all summoned back to school. Karelia explained that *la revolución* had assigned us an important political task: to welcome foreigners who were in Cuba for the Pan-American Games. "They have long legs and pale cheeks," the Pioneer guide informed us. "Sometimes they carry backpacks and wear sunglasses."

We would greet them with a short speech, "Good morning, comrade. I am a Pioneer. In the name of the Cuban people, I welcome you to the homeland of Fidel and José Martí. I hope you enjoy Havana and the conquests of our revolution. Would you mind signing my Pan-American guest book?"

"The three students who collect the most signatures will receive prizes," Karelia added, encouragingly.

"What kind of prizes?" Marlene asked with a yawn that mirrored the general discontent. No one wanted to spend vacation time chasing long-legged foreigners in the streets.

"A month in Tarará for the first place, and bicycles for three runners up."

Marlene's face brightened.

"Now, don't forget to wear the red kerchiefs and the berets. And for Lenin's sake, iron your blouses and shirts!"

"I can't fit into my uniform anymore," Sonia whispered to me. "And *Mamá* isn't going to buy me another since we'll have to use a different one in middle school."

"If a foreigner asks if life in Cuba is hard, say 'no'," Karelia warned us. "Even if we now have some minor difficulties, they are not to be discussed with strangers. These people come from richer countries and may misinterpret things. We have to make *El Comandante* look good."

Sonia and I stood on the corner of Infanta Avenue and San Lázaro Street. She had written down our welcoming speech.

"My memory is terrible," she said. "I don't want to make a *papelazo*."

Making a *papelazo* was embarrassing oneself in the worst possible way. She just did when she approached a young guy who wore a pair of stylish sunglasses. He listened to her and laughed, "You thought I was a foreigner? I'm going after those dudes myself. Come with me and I'll teach you how to offer something better than blah-blah-blah."

When we finally got hold of a paled-faced and sandal-clad foreign couple, their response was giving us chewing gum and a small Canadian flag. They walked away yelling, "Long life to Fidel! Down with Yankee imperialism!"

Along came an overweight man. He hugged us—longer than necessary. And he smelled badly. He scribbled "*Vivan los Juegos Panamericanos*!" in Sonia's guest book and left. No more foreigners passed by. Sweaty and bored, I gave up. "Forget the signatures and let's go home," I said.

"Are you crazy? I want to go back to Tarará! There

is nothing to eat at home. Yesterday *Mamá* only gave us a hard boiled egg and two slices of bread for dinner. And Mónica, my little sister, just turned seven years old and lost her ration-card milk."

You-know-who had asked Cubans "to share their resources with the athletes and comrades who attended the Pan-American Games." That meant that our rations were reduced even more.

An hour later Sonia suggested we sign the guest books ourselves. We just had to be careful and disguise our handwriting, making it look as "foreign" as possible. On the way back to Carlos III Avenue we met a group of Guatemalans that provided her with seven authentic signatures and a poster of Rigoberta Menchú. Sonia took it to her apartment to cover a crack on the *barbacoa* peeling walls.

Karelia praised my friend's efforts. The principal gave her a Cuban flag pin and a T-shirt with the Games' mascot, a scrawny bird called Cocopán.

§ § §

My parents had agreed the Papucho could take me out anytime but I was to return to our apartment at night. I couldn't sleep in Grandma Rosa's place, Ma mère explained, because the room was packed now that Flor lived there too. I hadn't met her yet and wasn't really looking forward to it.

"All stepmothers are bitches," Sonia told me. "From Cinderella's and Snow White's to my father's new wife. I don't trust any of them."

Papucho didn't have a visiting schedule. He would come by five days in a row and then disappear for three weeks. He was often behind in child support payments. We were used to that, but when six weeks passed without news from him, Ma mère got anxious. "If he doesn't show up this weekend, we'll have to go to Los Pinos and pick up the money," she said. "I bet he's already spent it on booze. He's so irresponsible!"

Sonia and I decided to wait for the Festival visitors around Malecón Drive, which was a livelier location than Infanta Avenue.

"Esbieta met a foreign guy yesterday, a Uruguayan," she said while we walked by the seawall. "He bought her a pair of shoes at the Riviera Hotel 'shopping' and chocolate bars for Mónica and me. But *Mamá* was furious and told my sister that she wouldn't allow her to be a *jinetera*."

"A what?"

"A dollar-zone hooker, *chica*."

"Esbieta is going to be a doctor. She has no need of becoming...that."

"Some young doctors are *jineteras* too. They make more money sleeping with foreigners than treating Cuban patients."

Sonia had to be joking. The only prostitutes I had encountered up to then were fictional characters, like my friend's namesake in *Crime and Punishment*.

"I thought there were no whores in Cuba anymore."

"Longina, open your eyes!" Sonia laughed. "Where have you been since the 'special period' began, girl?"

§ § §

The Pan-American Games were in full swing. *Granma* published interviews with promising athletes. Mayito González, a handsome Cuban swimmer, became an instant celebrity after winning his first gold medal. Havana's mood was festive...in a fake sort of way. People cheered *los Juegos Panamericanos* in the meetings organized by the Committees for the Defense of the Revolution and hung flags from their balconies. But they cursed You-know-who under their breath, in the bread waiting lines and in front of the empty *carnicerías*.

Sonia and I went signature-seeking every morning. Near *La Fiat*, a dollar-zone cafeteria, we met a middle-aged American with her hair pulled in two pigtails under a Cocopán cap.

"Is it true that Cubans can't get off the island without the government's authorization?" she asked in a haltering Spanish, after a few minutes of polite, apolitical chat.

"We don't know about that," Sonia said. But I nodded.

"I heard in Miami that young professionals can't leave the country," the woman went on.

"That's right!" I replied. "The emigration department never allowed my parents to leave."

Ignoring Sonia's hard stares, I began to tell her about our denied exit permits. But I didn't get to finish the story. The American cut me off in mid-sentence.

"I can't understand why anyone would want to leave a country where people have everything!" she yelled. "Look at yourselves, receiving free education while I have to pay for my kids' college in the United States! You really *shouldn't* want to leave your homeland but love it and pay attention to Fidel. Listen to *El Comandante*. He will someday destroy the Yankee Empire!"

Her high-pitched voice scared us so badly that we ran away without even asking for a signature.

The weekend passed. And Papucho? Fine, *gracias*. As elusive as a sirloin steak. Ma mère persuaded Orozco to use his last gallons of gas and take us to Los Pinos. We left behind the El Vedado avenues, decked out with Pan-American Games posters and Cuban flags, and drove through poorly lit streets where people stopped to look at the Lada.

As usual, a river of rumba and salsa flooded the tenement. Ma mère and I walked down the hall avoiding puddles of dirty water, a trashcan that smelled of rotten fish, and a headless chicken tied with a red ribbon. Only a true Santería believer would throw away a whole chicken in our "special period" circumstances!

No one answered when I knocked at Grandma Rosa's door. We were ready to leave when an officious neighbor approached us. "Are you looking for Rosa, Papucho and Flor?" she asked.

"Yes, yes."

"They left a month ago. Dangerous, eh, with the kind of weather we had then. I hope they made it," she added in a conspiratorial tone.

She didn't mention the words "raft" and "Miami" but they were understood.

"Did he give you the money?" Orozco asked when we went back to the car.

Instead of answering Ma mère burst into tears, asking for *San* Millán de la Cogolla's help.

"*Ya, mujer, ya*," Orozco tried to console her when he finally found out what had happened. "Calm down. The three of them are in Miami now, for sure. I bet that your ex knew how to make a good, proper boat."

I thought that *Orejón* was glad to get rid of Papucho, once and for all. But he was also a gracious winner, not even voicing a *comecandela* reproach.

As we drove back to Carlos III Avenue, I tried to imagine my father's "proper boat" but couldn't. He was a stonemason, not a carpenter. And there were waves, sharks, coastguards...

Se fue para no volver,
Se fue sin decirme adiós.

Why had Papucho left without saying goodbye? Hadn't he ever loved me? I cried myself to sleep, like the day Ma mère had ordered him to "get out of our lives." It was the second time I lost my father, and I suspected it would be the last.

"You have to be more careful, *chica*," Sonia warned me after the incident with the American. "If that broad had denounced us for badmouthing 'this,' we'd be in trouble now. These foreigners are all *comecandelas* and don't want to hear about our problems."

I learned to keep my mouth shut, and to open it only to sing *El Comandante*'s praises. Oh, yes, Cuba was a socialist paradise, I answered with my sweetest smile. Blackouts? They were a thing of the past. Food? All we could ask for. And we were allowed to travel freely to Patagonia if we wished...Not all the visitors seemed convinced. A young Argentinean guy, in a typical poncho, asked if Cubans were afraid to speak their minds. Sonia and I denied it.

"No, comrade," I stated firmly. "We aren't afraid of anything."

"How could we be?" Sonia added with a grin. "Don't you know that *El Comandante* watches over us?"

She got a kick out of lying with a straight face to the serious-looking, funny-accented adults who listened to us respectfully.

"But they are going to think we are idiots!" I told her.

"So? We'll never see them again. And no one is going to beat me out of that Tarará vacation."

She had collected over two hundred signatures, plus the ones we had counterfeited.

"What about Esbieta's boyfriend?" I asked. "Are they still going out?"

"Every night. He took her to Cayo Coco, a tourist-only resort. But *Mamá* is so mad that she isn't speaking to Esbieta anymore. She can't stand the guy."

"Esbieta has had other boyfriends before and your mom hasn't cared. What's wrong with him? She doesn't like foreigners or what?"

"Nothing is wrong with him and she does like foreigners. Only that he's fifty years old and—"

"Fifty? But Esbieta isn't twenty yet!"

"Are you going to be old fashioned too? Who cares how old he is? He has dollars, get it? And he can take her to every 'shopping' in Cuba and buy her blouses, perfumes, frozen chicken, soap. . . Where is she going to go that she's worth more? The only thing she has to do is—well—please him."

"How?"

"In bed, *chica*. Wake up!"

Sex had become an alluring subject now that many of my friends, among them Sonia, were already *señoritas*. In normal times I would have spent hours thinking of Sonia's pretty sister and her elderly boyfriend. But I was too concerned for Papucho. I was also worried about Grandma Rosa, though I had never been as close to her as I was to Muñeca.

"A letter from Papucho will arrive soon," my grandma comforted me. "*La Yuma* mail is very slow."

"But why doesn't he call?"

"Because...because phone calls from Miami are expensive and he may not have enough money yet."

The look in her tired eyes, surrounded by a pictogram of wrinkles, betrayed her. She was lying, as Sonia and I did to the naïve foreigners who questioned us. She didn't believe that Papucho had reached Miami. And in my heart, I didn't either. He would have called me already, wouldn't he?

Ma mère and I began to listen to Radio Martí in Ponciano's old radio. Messages from the *balseros* were read every night. But many rafts reached the Florida shores empty, like one that had the names of seven people—an entire family—scratched on the battered wood...

My resentment against "this" deepened. Why couldn't we travel abroad like all the Pan-American Games guests? Why did Cubans have to leave on rafts, secretly, while foreigners took planes? And why, on top of everything, did we have to pretend we lived in paradise?

The Cuban national anthem. Cheering crowds. Mayito González proudly showing his gold medal. Kids dressed like Cocopán. The last images of the 11th Pan-American Games were eclipsed by Papucho's face, thin and craggy as the last time I had seen it. Was he already in Miami? Maybe Flor didn't allow him to call. Maybe he was drunk. Maybe he was—dead.

"The games were indeed a victory of *la revolución*," Orozco said, his eyes fixed on the black-and-white TV screen. "But I'm afraid that our economy wasn't ready to afford such an expense," he added, scratching his head. "The country spent millions of pesos in three weeks and beans haven't come to the grocery store for the last two months."

Politics can't be stuffed inside the sugar bowl.

Military marches. *El Comandante* shaking the champions' hands. Men and women holding Che Guevara banners, beer bottles, Cuban flags. Papucho's face again. Had he drowned? Was it my mother's fault? He wouldn't have left if she hadn't dumped him. I was mad at her. And I was mad at him, too. What a father, who hadn't even had the decency to say goodbye to me...

Who was to blame? Ma mère? Orozco? Papucho's drinking? Perestroika? Myself?

§ § §

Our class met for the last time in the Ho Chi Minh School. The prospect of the Tarará trip and the promised bicycles had created an atmosphere of joyful expectation, but I couldn't share it. The following year Sonia and I wouldn't be in the same classroom. She had already chosen a middle school in Centro Habana, but Ma mère wanted to enroll me at a distant boarding school. Except for the brief Tarará experience, I had always lived at home and was afraid of the new life that awaited me in seventh grade.

Karelia praised our revolutionary commitment. She encouraged us to be good comrades and not to forget the school and our old teachers. She didn't mention the rewards, though, and Sonia started getting fidgety.

"Have a great summer, kids," the Pioneer guide said, and looked relieved as a few students walked away.

"Wait a moment!" Marlene stood up and faced Karelia. "What about the prizes, *eh*?"

"Which—which prizes?"

"Tarará and the bicycles! I got three hundred signatures!"

"And I got four hundred and ten!" Sonia showed her Pan-American Games guest book as if it were a gold medal. "*Miren*!"

More kids produced their guest books, yelling at the top of their lungs. The classroom turned into a beehive. Karelia hung her head.

"I am sorry, pioneers," she said. "The superintendent just told me that we didn't have money for bicycles. The country spent too much on the Pan-American Games. We are broke."

"But Tarará...," Marlene insisted.

"Tarará is now the Chernobyl Project and will be reserved for Ukrainian children," Karelia looked at the disappointed faces that surrounded her and repeated, "I'm sorry. I wish I could send you all there. But it wasn't my fault."

We left quietly. Thirty Pan-American Games guest books, torn apart, carpeted the halls of the Ho Chi Minh Elementary School.

Chapter 3

The great blue house. Vocational School Vladimir Ilyich Lenin. Or just *La Lenin*. This was the place that became my new home when I started seventh grade. An elite boarding school inaugurated by Leonid Brezhnev in 1974, *La Lenin* was one of You-know-who's pet projects. It received special attention, and funding, even during the "special period."

A banner that read "Eternal glory to Vladimir Ilyich Lenin" and a bust of the Bolsheviks' leader welcomed visitors at the entrance. Another banner praising the indestructible friendship between Cuba and the Soviet Union had been removed in 1990, another casualty of perestroika.

Almost all the *La Lenin* graduates went to college. College was still in my distant future, but Ma mère had set her heart on sending me to the boarding school. She reminded me constantly of the black mark in my permanent record, though she chose to forget why I had gotten it in the first place. Students with *gusano* behavior were not admitted at the University of Havana. "Besides, you need to broaden your horizons," she said. "That will not happen if you go to a dingy Centro Habana school."

Orozco acted as if he had nothing to do with the *La Lenin* plan, but he was clearly behind it. Thanks to his contacts I got admitted, despite my marred record.

The first two months at *La Lenin* were hard. I pleaded with Ma mère every weekend to let me register at a local secondary school. Muñeca lobbied for me in vain. I should be grateful for the opportunity to mingle with the future leaders of Cuba, my mother and Orozco said.

All of *El Comandante*'s sons had studied at *La Lenin*. Jorge Lezcano's daughter and Ramiro Valdez's grandson were enrolled there. But they paid no attention to me. And I wouldn't have dared to approach them in class nor at the school parties where the presence of bodyguards was as common as meringue cakes, imported sausages and fruit juices. The food issue was another argument that Ma mère used ad nauseam. Wasn't I eating better than at home? She was right. Though the *La Lenin* meals weren't of gourmet quality, at least we didn't go to bed hungry.

La Lenin had sprawling green areas (the most popular was el *Bosque de la Amistad,* better known as the making-out forest), a modern chemistry lab and an Olympic-size pool. We wore blue shirts and berets, nicer than the ugly mustard uniforms used by regular middle-school students. And we were in a blackout-free zone.

But I still didn't like it. The offspring of high-ranking military officers, *mayimbes*, ruled the place. *La Lenin* was plagued by cliques: children of generals, of Politburo members, of diplomats and of the emerging dollar-zone class formed by hotel and "shopping" managers... An ordinary Centro Habana girl was an outsider there.

My roommates were Bratislava and Miroslava Cárdenas, daughters of a five-star general who stood next to You-know-who during his televised speeches. Bratislava was tall and trim, with a commanding presence. She often contradicted our Marxism teacher, who was too intimidated by her father's status to argue with her. Miroslava was clownish, short and stocky, and favored pastries over politics.

Tatiana Fresno and Lisaveta Miralles also shared our room. The granddaughter of the Cuban ambassador to the United Nations, Tatiana had *malas pulgas,* a notorious bad temper. She once broke the front teeth of a boy who had "looked at her in an improper way." Lisaveta, the daughter of a Prensa Latina journalist, had lived in Romania for eight years. They all spoke at least two languages, while I could hardly say *merde* and *au revoir* in French. Among such well-traveled kids I felt lowly and unsophisticated, a *pobrecita* who hadn't even visited the east provinces of Cuba or the Isle of Youth.

At school I sat next to Aliosha. He had grown up in Moscow, where his father was a cultural attaché. But he hated his name and his upbringing. "Call me Alex," he asked me the first day. "I can't stand a name that sounds just like a girl's."

Alex got into fights when others said he was a *bolo*, a pejorative term used to refer to Soviets. But, roly-poly and red-haired, he didn't look like a Cuban at all. His Spanish was poor and he mixed it with Russian, occasionally reverting to the Cyrillic alphabet. We became friends after our grammar teacher, in desperation, asked me to tutor him. In return, Alex taught me a few useful things, like French kissing, later on... Lisaveta struggled with her Spanish too. After seven years at the Budapest Soviet School, she was taking classes in her native language for the first time. "I hate irregular verbs," she said. "You can't even put them in a list, as they do in English."

Many of my classmates were "shoppings" patrons. Boys showed off in Ray Ban sunglasses and Polo shirts. Girls smelled like Oscar De La Renta and Estée Lauder fragrances. They discussed the quality and prices of the merchandise sold at *Quinta y Cuarenta y Dos*, a dollar-zone supermarket located at the corner of 5th and 42nd Avenues, and at chic boutiques like *La Maison*. *Mayimbe* daughters were *las chicas del swing*, the cool gals.

To the school parties *las chicas del swing* wore T-shirts that advertised foreign rock groups, beer brands or baseball teams. They strutted around in denim miniskirts and American jeans. Oh, those fabulous Levis, faded and with big holes like hungry mouths at knee level! And yet they weren't super cool. The *La Lenin* queen was the niece of a deposed Latin American leftist president. Her family traveled to Europe every summer. She disdained our "shoppings," bought her clothes at *El Corte Inglés*, in Spain, and collected *Hola* and *Vogue* issues. But the most sought-after publication was a tattered *Playboy* magazine, property of the Minister of Culture's son.

§ § §

The *La Lenin* halls had the usual Marx, Lenin and Che Guevara posters, peppered with revolutionary slogans. But from the bedroom walls Madonna, Raphael and U2 grinned at *El Comandante*'s ideological heirs. The bathrooms were kept clean and supplied with toilet paper, though we had to bring soap from home. I was lucky; the Cárdenas girls loaned me Palmolive bars and, in emergencies, Colgate toothpaste.

Students lived at *La Lenin* Monday through Friday. We went to school in the mornings and worked in the afternoons at a battery factory. This way we followed the revolutionary rule of combining work and study. My brigade packed dry batteries in cardboard boxes. It wasn't hard labor, but we snubbed it and spent the afternoons chatting and playing. That is, when we didn't sneak out to the nearby Botanical Garden or return to *La Lenin* on our own. The overseers smiled and pretended not to notice. Our supervisor once said to another worker, "Don't mess with the *La Lenin* kids. One never knows who is the child, legitimate or not, of a *mayimbe*."

We had dinner at seven and free time until ten-thirty, when lights were officially turned off. But they stayed on, in the dorms, until eleven or midnight. As long as we didn't make too much noise, the teachers didn't bother us. They slept in separate rooms and adhered to the same politics as the factory overseers.

The Cárdenas sisters owned a Panasonic radio and listened to Miami stations every night. Miroslava liked music and was a fan of Gloria Estefan. Lisaveta preferred political programs. Sometimes she managed to pick up Radio Martí, despite the Cuban government's interference.

"These are the same *teques* we hear at school, just of the opposite side," Miroslava complained.

Teques were boring political discourses like those we had to put up with in the Marxism seminars.

"Yes, but there are a few facts in the Radio Martí *teques*," Lisaveta replied. "Ours are always full of...how do you say it in Spanish? Blah-blah-blah!"

Students sometimes brought cassettes with foreign music to the school parties. The teachers initially protested when we learned to dance the lambada. They labeled it indecent and bourgeois. Then they learned it as well. *Chorando se foi* (He left crying) by Kaoma was a hit for several months.

When I finished seventh grade, Orozco and his ex-wife finally reached an agreement. She would keep their home and give him twenty thousand pesos in exchange for his right to it. The money would help us to make a good *permuta*, trading our apartment for a big house in El Vedado or Miramar.

That was *Orejón*'s idea. He wanted a place ample enough for his children to stay during the weekends. A garage was a plus, now that car thefts had doubled. The apartment alone couldn't get us into a house like that, but the equivalent of four hundred dollars would surely make a difference, he said. (A dollar cost fifty pesos on the black market.) It was still illegal to offer money in *permutas* but, in this case, Orozco was willing to forfeit his communist principles. That was his personal version of perestroika at home.

I felt again like the ghost-fearful girl who didn't want to leave San Anastasio Street. How was I going to keep in touch with my Centro Habana friends, particularly Sonia? She didn't have a phone, "camels" passed every two hours and regular buses were now extinct. Moving again meant uprooting once more and I had had enough of that. It wasn't fair, I told Muñeca. Not fair at all.

She agreed, but her influence on family life had diminished considerably. She wasn't *la mandamás* anymore. Ma mère and Orozco made all the important decisions, like trading houses or sending me to a boarding school. Muñeca wasn't even consulted. "That's why I never wanted to be an old woman," she complained.

Orozco's kids were six and nine years old and had inherited their father's elephant ears. Why did I have to see them every weekend? Why did I have to share my mother and Muñeca with them? And my food and my books and my space? *No jodan*!

To make things worse, Orozco was becoming preachy. After Ponciano's death he got more vocal about his political views and even attempted to "convert" Muñeca and me. His proselytizing started right when the socialist world that he had believed in began to crumble. He was probably losing his own faith, my grandma said, and thought that if he could instill it in others, it would return to him. Fat chance.

But Ma mère, the perpetual chameleon, was already a *comecandela*. Or pretended to be. With her, one never knew.

"Some women are like sponges," Sonia said. "Esbieta is now involved with a guy from Quebec so she fakes a French accent and calls me *ma chère soeur*."

The Canadian was old enough to be Esbieta's grandfather, but this time around her mother didn't protest. Rumor had it that our pretty neighbor had quietly joined the *jinetera* scene. She dropped out of college and didn't work, but dressed like a *La Yuma* actress. She had already had several short-term partners, all foreigners and over fifty.

"Is she majoring in international relations?" Avelina asked with an impertinent smile.

"People are just envious," Sonia defended her sister. "It isn't Esbieta's fault that mature foreigners like her. And they resolve a lot, more than Cuban men."

The word "resolving" now meant getting staples like cooking oil, milk, meat and soap that couldn't be found in peso-zone stores anymore. Proof of the foreign guys' abilities to "resolve" things were the Jordache jeans Sonia was wearing, her watch with a Betty Boop face and the rice cooker that occupied the place of honor in their recently painted apartment.

"Esbieta also has a Cuban boyfriend," Sonia confessed, "A handsome touristaxi driver. He's twenty-five years old and adores her. But he knows that he has to let her earn a living."

Jineteras, resolving, *cerelac*, touristaxis... Our daily vocabulary kept reinventing itself and people did the same while You-know-who tried to stuff politics inside the sugar bowl.

During the Friday night blackouts Orozco sat in the

living room and made *comecandela* overtures, mostly directed to Muñeca and me. One warm May evening, when the first flies began to buzz around the hurricane lamp, he opened fire, "I read in *Granma* that power shortages are over. A Chinese oil tanker is coming to Havana next month, and maybe a Vietnamese ship with canned meat. We are lucky that socialism is still alive."

"Before socialism" Muñeca replied, "we never had blackouts and there was fresh meat in abundance."

"But not for everyone," he unsuccessfully tried to catch a fly that kept charging against his forehead.

"And the poor people in the countryside didn't have electricity at all," Ma mère added.

The fly was now on my grandma's nose.

"Blackouts are caused by the Yankee blockade," Orozco said. "The Americans don't allow other countries to sell us oil."

Comecandelas said blockade. *Gusanos* preferred embargo.

"There are blackout-free zones in Miramar," Muñeca said. "Do you think that Raúl Castro and You-know-who are sitting in the dark, eating crap and catching flies like us? *No jodas*! Why doesn't the embargo have the same effect on everybody?"

She swatted the fly.

"Well, *El Comandante* and his family. . . ," Orozco stuttered. "They aren't like us. They need to be protected."

"Protected from what?"

"From the CIA. If Fidel lived in a neighborhood affected by blackouts, imperialist agents would plant a bomb there. They have tried to kill him, to poison our crops, to..."

"*Ay*, Orozco!" my grandma exploded. "When you have diarrhea, do you also blame the CIA for it?"

Orozco waited until Muñeca went to the balcony "to get some fresh air," as she said. Then he turned toward me, "When are you going to become a Young Communist, Longina? The sooner you start the application process, the better."

Two days before Lisaveta had compared the Young Communist League to Hitler's Youth, after watching a program on the fall of Nazism. The Marxism teacher, horrified, had sent her to the principal's office.

"Our country is going through difficult times," Orozco went on, "And young revolutionaries like you are..."

"I am not in the mood for *teques*, okay?" I snapped, joining my grandma on the balcony.

Ma mère sighed. Orozco went after another fly and Muñeca squeezed my hand.

Yes, I listened to enough *comecandela* speeches at school. But it was also at *La Lenin* where I heard, for the first time, unveiled criticism of the system and even of You-know-who. My classmates didn't just whisper about "this." They used familiarly the first names of our leaders, criticized them and discussed the possibility of a revolt in Cuba, an aftereffect of the movement that had changed the European map.

"Would Raúl order the troops to fire on the crowds as Ceausescu did in Romania?" Miroslava asked once.

"I don't doubt it," Lisaveta answered. "Raúl is a coward, always hiding behind his brother's shadow."

"Juan wouldn't, for sure," Miroslava smirked. "He's too busy with girls and *musiquita*."

Juan Almeida Bosque, a Commander of the Revolution who had fought at the Sierra Maestra Mountains, was better known for his interest in starlets and music.

"Most *mayimbes* will support a new leader," Bratislava said. "My dad thinks that Fidel is too old and should just step down. But even the generals are scared now.

Remember what happened to Arnaldo?

General Arnaldo Ochoa, a former Hero of the Republic and an Angola veteran, had been accused of drug trafficking and executed in 1989. Many believed that he was actually planning to overthrow You-know-who.

"Arnaldo left supporters," Lisaveta said.

Something in her tone implied that she was one of them. Lisaveta wasn't a *chica del swing*. Her curly hair, always tucked under a baseball cap, and her ragged tennis shoes gave her a hippie-like, defiant air.

"And he has spiritual followers who pray to him," Miroslava added. "Arnaldo is now in Santería altars, next to Tony the Twin."

Colonel Tony de La Guardia, also accused of drug dealing, had been executed with Ochoa. His twin brother, Patricio, went to prison, where he still was. In Santería, the *orishas* called Ibeyes are regarded as sacred twins and *santeros* said that the De La Guardia brothers were under their protection.

"Too bad that they are dead," she concluded.

"No one else has *cojones* enough to do a thing against the Bearded One," Bratislava said, after a long pause. "I wonder if we wouldn't be better off in another country. . ."

Lisaveta cut her off, "If everyone leaves, who will change 'this'? We have to bring perestroika to Cuba instead!"

"*Viva* glasnost!" Miroslava yelled.

I wanted to tell Orozco all that, just to see him scowl. But I was also afraid of a confrontation that forced Ma mère to take sides. I'd rather keep the hope that I was more important to her than her new husband's political views.

There were *comecandela* kids at school, though it wasn't cool to be one. Often the relationship between a student's opposition to "this" and his or her family revolutionary status was inversely proportional.

Yania Yarmila was a *comecandela.* She didn't have *mayimbe* relatives but was admitted in *La Lenin* because of her own political commitment. A classroom leader since the fourth grade, she had already applied to the Young Communist League. She had a collection of stuffed Mishas, the Moscow Olympic Games mascot, and still sang *Katiuska* sentimentally. Miroslava teased her and wrote obscene messages, in Russian, on her notebooks.

But Alex, Lisaveta and the Cárdenas girls agreed that communism was doomed. They supported their views with examples from the ex-socialist countries where they had lived. Bratislava quoted Milan Kundera. Lisaveta rooted for Lech Walesa and used terms like "market economy" that I had never heard.

I kept to myself at first, fearing that I had little in common with my sophisticated classmates. But my concerns disappeared by the second semester. These kids weren't like Barbarita or Orozco, who worshipped *El Comandante* as if he were a distant, omnipotent and omnipresent god. The *La Lenin* kids called Fidel You-know-who or The Bearded One and even made fun of him.

"He doesn't deliver long speeches anymore because he's getting old and his voice cracks in the middle of a three-hour *teque,*" said Alex.

"Or because he has to pee halfway through it!" Miroslava replied.

Lisaveta was my first *La Lenin* friend. I helped her with Spanish grammar assignments and she told me about the foreign lands she had seen. Her family had traveled all over Europe, a privilege reserved for loyal Fidelists like her father. (Or like her father used to be, because now he was a perestroika supporter, she admitted.) Lisaveta wouldn't brag about her trips, clothes or shopping sprees, but discussed foreign newspaper articles. She didn't collect fashion magazines, favoring "serious" ones like *Le Monde* and *The Atlantic Monthly*.

She once brought to school a copy of the Declaration of Human Rights. "A subversive, bourgeois and counterrevolutionary document," the teachers and Orozco said. But she kept showing it all over *La Lenin* until the Marxism instructor confiscated the crumpled, photocopied pages, and put a disciplinary note in her file. "He may as well put it up his fat ass," was her only comment.

One evening we were herded to the School Theater to watch a video of You-know-who's latest speech. The principal met with us before.

"The content of the speech is still classified matter," he said. "You can't repeat to anybody what you are going to hear tonight."

The Cárdenas girls yawned. It would be another *teque* about *la guerra de todo el pueblo*, Bratislava said. But she was wrong. Instead, You-know-who talked at length of the "zero option" that Cuba might be facing soon if the economy failed to improve. "Zero option" meant zero energy, zero oil, zero supplies. Above all, zero hope. A permanent, programmed blackout.

Cuban cities would fade away, he prophesied. The country would resort to primitive agriculture, hoe and oxen included. That would be advantageous since oxen didn't hurt the soil the way modern tractors did, he emphasized gravely, shaking his index finger. The ration card would disappear because everybody would eat from communal kitchens. Dollar and peso shops would also close. All the schools would move to the countryside, most likely to the east provinces, and we would become student-farmers.

There were no applauses at the end, as it was customary when we watched this televised speeches. The teachers were somber and the kids furious or scared. Even Yania Yarmila looked frightened.

"Where does he think we are, in Cambodia?" Lisaveta asked as we left the theater. I didn't know what she was talking about. What did Cambodia have to do with "zero option?" She went on, "The *cabrón* is always blaming the Yankees for our lack of resources, but never mentions all the money that foreigners spend at hotels, tourist-only resorts and dollar shops. Transparency is what we need here, not oxen!"

"Keep your voice down," I told her, noticing that the principal was around. He was a Lilliputian man with a titan's ego.

"I am not going to shut up!" Lisaveta gave the finger to the principal or maybe to an invisible You-know-who. "People in other countries are using the World Wide Web and he wants Cuba to go back to the Stone Age!"

"I am not moving to any damned countryside!" Alex shouted.

"Me neither!" Bratislava said. "*Qué* oxen *ni qué carajo*!"

Miroslava started to sing, "The people have the right to party..."

The principal walked away. He probably didn't like the idea of being sent, hoe in hand, to a remote province either.

"I think we should get out of here," Bratislava whispered on our way to the dorms, "before 'this' becomes worse."

"But why?" replied Lisaveta, "Why should *we* go?

He's the one who messed up the country. We ought to kick *him* out!"

"But how?"

Once in our room Bratislava turned on the radio. She couldn't pick up Radio Martí and resorted to the Voice of America. The *Yankee Doodle* tune filled the room and brought Ponciano's shadow to the edge of my bunk bed. What would he have said about "zero option"?

Lisaveta told me about thc Khmer Rouge and its tactics of displacement. Then she outlined her plans for a new Cuba where she would be the first woman president. With that, I fell asleep.

Chapter 4

Pioneer City had disappeared. First Tarará turned into the Chernobyl Project, a recovery resort for Ukrainian children affected by the nuclear plant explosion. When Cuban kids stayed, their parents had to bring food, dishes and even bedclothes from home.

The early nineties brought about another transformation. Tarará became a dollar-zone town. Cubans weren't allowed in the restored Art Deco villas unless a foreigner went with them and paid for their stay. *Jineteras*, not much older than the students who used to vacation there before the "special period," became regular guests at the resort. Security guards patrolled the place constantly. Pancho's job was now to keep unauthorized Cubans away.

The reward for outstanding Pioneers was a week in a *Campismo Popular* site, a desolate place with no cafeterias, restrooms or potable water nearby. Mónica, Sonia's younger sister, returned from a *Campismo Popular* trip constipated and full of lice. "We ate green bananas for breakfast, lunch and dinner," she whined.

Esbieta convinced her latest "boyfriend," a sixty-two year old Spaniard, to rent a villa in Tarará. She took Sonia and Mónica with them. "It's much better now than when we went," Sonia told me after they returned suntanned, happy and plump. "We ate at a different restaurant every night. Nothing was rationed. And remember the old ceiling fan that didn't work? Our house had air conditioning, a color TV set in each bedroom, and a microwave in the kitchen."

"What's a microwave?"

"Sort of a plastic oven that heats food instantly. An

American wonder, *chica*. Old Pepe is going to buy one for my mom."

I envied her. No one in my immediate family knew how to "resolve" things. And I was saddled with a couple of nosey stepbrothers who spoiled my weekends at home. Poor me.

That was how I presented the situation to my friends, with the face of a martyr. Actually, Orozco's kids weren't too annoying. When they visited, they played baseball in the Carlos III Avenue Park or pestered their father to teach them how to drive. I made a point of ignoring them and they didn't mess with me. But still, they were on my turf, and I resented it.

Some weekends I didn't return home. I instead went to a beach house that the Cárdenas family had in Guanabo. Communist Party leaders, ambassadors and *mayimbes* had the right to vacation in former bourgeois houses now known as *casas de descanso*. The Cárdenas had been assigned a mansion with six bedrooms and a swimming pool in the backyard.

Ma mère always gave me permission to stay at the beach house. Maybe Orozco had convinced her that a general's daughters were the best company for me. But my absences made Muñeca sad. "Please, come back this weekend," she begged me every Monday morning. "You are my sunshine. No one else cares for this old woman anymore."

General Cárdenas and his wife were out of Cuba—on a perestroika-related mission, Bratislava revealed. The girls organized sleepovers and invited their *La Lenin* friends, who never turned them down. Emilia, the housekeeper, kept the refrigerator stuffed with imported cheese, lobster, cured ham, Coca Cola bottles and other delicacies from "shoppings" and dollar-zone restaurants.

She cooked for us and was a cross between maid and chaperone. Boys visited during the day but Emilia didn't let them stay after dark.

"If *las niñas* get in trouble, General Cárdenas will kill me," she said.

"But we can also get in trouble at *La Lenin*," Miroslava replied. "The making-out forest is available all the time."

"You know better than that, Miss Smart Ass."

Miroslava, Bratislava and even Lisaveta were less "liberated" than Centro Habana girls like Marlene and Esbieta. In sexual matters they behaved more like old fashioned aristocratic girls from the pre-*Comandante* times.

It was at the beach house where I first saw *Repentance*. Lisaveta had brought the video and insisted we watch it, causing a general protest.

"A *bolo* movie?" Miroslava shrieked. "You're crazy! Puah!"

All the Soviet films we knew were boring war dramas or unabashed propaganda. A title like *Repentance* didn't offer much hope. We only agreed to see it when Lisaveta explained, "The movie was shown three weeks ago at the Yara Theater, but *Seguridad* agents forbade it after the second day."

The reviews published in the newspapers *Granma* and *Juventud Rebelde* helped people decide which film to watch by the law of contraries. If the comments were favorable, the movie theater was as bare as a grocery store shelf. But if the critics mentioned the "ideological weakness of the plot" or "the director's decadent points of view" lines at the box office were three blocks long.

Repentance had been cut to ribbons by the *Granma* reviewers. No wonder we loved it. Lisaveta clapped as Keti announced, "Varlam will not rest. The sentence is final." Miroslava smiled at the baked cakes and I cried quietly when the piles of logs scratched by prisoners arrived at the train station. They reminded me of the empty raft that had reached the Miami shores carrying a silent message from the *balseros* swallowed by the sea. . .

We all understood why the movie had been prohibited. Wasn't the dead dictator You-know-who's carbon copy?

"Cubans need to find the road to the temple," Lisaveta said pensively.

"They have already found it," Miroslava laughed. "It's called 'Miami Way.'"

Lisaveta's face got red. "That's not funny, you know? Why does everybody only think about leaving? Doesn't the homeland mean anything?"

"Yes, it means...," Miroslava flashed her middle finger, "'this!'"

§ § §

By the end of my second *La Lenin* year I wouldn't have been caught dead at a Centro Habana middle school. A proud resident of *La Gran Casa Azul*, I had made new friends there and "broadened my horizons." Where else would I have learned so much about perestroika? Ma mère had been right after all.

The economic situation had improved slightly. In a July 26th speech You-know-who made it legal for Cubans to own dollars. The government opened houses of exchange and American currency began to circulate freely, dropping its value to twenty-five pesos for one dollar. The "shoppings" weren't forbidden territory anymore, though the natives had to show their money to the security guards so as to be allowed inside. Browsing wasn't permitted.

Despite a façade of tolerance, things hadn't really changed *that* much. Luisito's mother, who lived in New York, fell ill. After finding out that she had an aggressive type of cancer, she begged to see her son one last time. The American consul gave Luisito a humanitarian visa to visit her for three months, though we all knew that he wouldn't return to Cuba. But when he asked for an exit permit, it was denied without any explanation. Two weeks later Luisito's mother died, and not even Muñeca could find words to console him. "I'll have to stay here forever," he said bitterly. "I'm doomed."

My family had moved but stayed in Centro Habana. To Orozco's disappointment, all El Vedado *permutantes* asked for at least one thousand dollars, or its equivalent in pesos. He didn't have that much. Our new home was in Zapata Street, close to Carlos III Avenue. It was an old house (though not as old as the one in Lawton) with an inner courtyard, a tiled hall and a covered front porch.

I had one of the four bedrooms to myself, even if I only used it on weekends. I needed privacy, Muñeca insisted. Over the summer vacation that followed my first year at *La Lenin* I had become a *señorita*. It was nothing extraordinary and I didn't experience the horrid pains that Sonia once predicted. Ma mère had bought in advance some sanitary towels—they were rationed, too—and taught me how to use them.

"I'm glad you are a woman, Longina," she told me. "But remember that you can produce babies now. Be careful around boys and men. You are too young to get involved, hear?"

"You don't need to worry about that," I said, shrugging.

I should have added "yet."

Because when the fall semester started, I found a boyfriend at *La Lenin*. It was Alex the *bolo*, who in a few months he had come out of his lard cocoon and become an excellent swimmer, a disciple of Mayito González. He had also acquired a sexy tan. School rules forbade us to lounge by the pool and get suntanned on purpose, which was considered a bourgeois habit. But he had gotten his tan honestly, after endless hours of training.

We hooked up due to a semantic slip. He had asked Lisaveta to let me know that he wanted to "be with me." That meant, in our slang, to be my boyfriend, *mi novio*. Lisaveta, who still had troubles with some verbs, turned it into "go out with me," and I accepted. That night Pablito Milanés was singing at the *La Lenin* amphitheater and I assumed that Alex just intended to accompany me to the concert.

After hearing other girls talk about their relationships, I wasn't in a hurry to get into one myself. The *apretadera*, the making out that went on in the *Bosque de la Amistad*, didn't tempt me. The French kiss business made me feel like puking. There were always the risks of pregnancy and AIDS, and I had promised my mother not to get involved.

Unfortunately, at eight o'clock Alex was waiting for me outside the girls' dorm with a dozen roses—he had asked his dad to bring them to school—a teddy bear and a postcard. "I'm so happy that you are now my girlfriend," he said and kissed me.

I cursed Lisaveta under my breath but didn't have

the heart to reject him. And he wasn't too bad for a first boyfriend. His Spanish had improved as much as his appearance and no one would call him a *bolo* anymore. Hand in hand, we headed for the concert. We sang together the sad tune of *Yolanda* and from that night on were *novios*.

Lisaveta's reputation as a matchmaker soared. But then she paired hoity-toity Tatiana with the conceited son of the Minister of Culture. They broke up after four days, but she kept trying to put people together.

"Why don't you get a guy for yourself?" I asked her.

"If I plan to be in public life, I need to be unencumbered," she answered. "But matchmaking is good practice for establishing future political alliances."

I wondered what Papucho would have said of Alex, but I didn't mention him to anyone at home. Not even to my grandma. Family *teques* were the last thing I wanted to hear.

Alex couldn't yet have a driver's license, but his father had taught him how to drive anyway. Cops didn't tend to stop cars with HK plates, an indication that their owners were foreigners or diplomats, so we were safe.

On Saturday evenings my boyfriend picked me up on the corner of Zapata Street and Carlos III Avenue. He drove to *El* Malecón and we made out in the back seat of his dad's Nissan. I found French kissing awkward and somewhat gross and never knew exactly what to do with my tongue. Elbows were a nuisance too. As for noses, I wished there were a convenient place to hide them. Mine seemed twice its size every time it touched Alex's face.

"This is not half as fun as people make it look," I confessed to Lisaveta.

Esbieta had managed to keep both the old Spaniard and the young touristaxi driver, Pavel Pérez. (He was, like her, a victim of the Soviet-name practice.) Sonia kept me current about her sister's adventures when I visited her on weekends.

One evening I came in when Esbieta was ready to go out. She looked gorgeous in a blue satin dress and six-inch high heels. And she smelled of Chanel N°5, a fragrance that brought memories of Ma mère in Papucho's times.

"You are so pretty!" I said. "I want to be twenty years old soon and look just like you!"

She smiled but didn't seem happy. "Well, I wish I were your age and looked like you now."

A car honked in the street. From the window, Sonia and I saw a white-haired man with a conspicuous belly get out of a Mercedes-Benz.

"Is he Pepe?" I asked, shocked. I knew the guy was old but not *that* old.

"Yes. We call him *El Abuelo* when Esbieta isn't around."

"Does she like him?"

"Of course not! She only likes Pavel. But yesterday Pepe asked her to marry him and go to Barcelona."

"What is she going to do in Barcelona, where she has no family or friends? She should marry Pavel instead."

"Pavel lives with his mother, his stepfather and two brothers. There is no space for another *barbacoa* in this apartment. Where are they going to sleep, in the bathroom? But if Esbieta goes to Spain she will have her own house, a maid, maybe even a car. One has to be practical, *chica*."

Finding a place of their own was impossible for young couples. Most in-laws refused to accept an additional mouth in their already crammed quarters. If I married Alex, I would probably have to live in his parents' Miramar home...which wasn't a bad idea, all things considered.

Sonia went on, "*Mamá* told Esbieta to say yes to Pepe and sign the papers as soon as possible, so *El Abuelo* doesn't have time to change his mind."

I remembered how upset their mother had been about the Uruguayan guy.

"Your mom has changed," I said.

"We all have changed."

"Will they get married here or in Spain?"

"Here. That's the only way she can get a Spanish visa. Esbieta will let me organize the wedding. And you are coming to the party! Who knows, we may find a couple of rich Spaniards for ourselves, too."

"Uh, thanks," the conversation was making me uncomfortable. "Want to go to Lisaveta's? She always has good videos."

"Uh, thanks!" Sonia mocked me. "You know I can't stand your *comecandela* pal."

My two best friends had clashed the first day we got together at Lisaveta's house.

"I missed Cuba so much when we lived in Romania," Lisaveta had said, "That I cried every time I saw our flag. I can't understand why people are so eager to leave. I'd never, ever go away again."

"It's easy for you to talk like that when your freezer is full of 'shopping' stuff," Sonia replied, examining with a resentful look the Miralles's living room, furnished with a leather sofa, a lacquered coffee table and a modern stereo system. "Mine resembles a coconut; it has nothing but water inside. I'd rather eat a steak than look at a damned flag."

Later Sonia maintained that Lisaveta was a *comecandela.* I explained to her that Lisaveta's love for Cuba had nothing to do with You-know-who, but she didn't believe me. For her, they were one and the same. Lisaveta, in turn, accused Sonia of being an unpatriotic bitch.

§ § §

On my weekends at home, I began to notice that Ma mère acted odd. She missed work. She vomited often, as I used to in the pre-Tarará days. She was tired all the time.

"What's wrong with her?" I asked Muñeca when I came from *La Lenin* one Friday afternoon and found Ma mère in bed at three P.M.

"Nothing," my grandma said. I shook my head and she added, "Thank God we have a bigger house now."

"Do you think she's pregnant?" I asked, horrified.

"Maybe, maybe...Don't repeat it, okay? She hasn't said anything yet but I know better."

"And she told me *I* had to be careful!" I burst out. "Look who ended up producing babies!"

Sonia confirmed Muñeca's suspicions. Her mother had had exactly the same symptoms the last time she was pregnant.

"The worst part comes after the baby is born," she informed me. "Then everything is for the newborn. Food, clothes, time, attention...The others become 'category B' kids. And you'll have to change diapers and clean dirty *culitos*!"

"Arf!"

"Why don't you try to convince her to get an abortion?"

I looked at Sonia, shocked. "*Chica*! I don't dare to do that."

"Esbieta has had several. It's nothing."

"But I really don't mind having a little brother or sister. The only problem is that Ma mère is so old... Thirty-seven, imagine that! What was she thinking?"

"She wasn't thinking, girl,"Sonia laughed."She was just having sex."

I couldn't fall asleep that night. Words and faces swirled in my mind dancing a wild lambada. Sex. My mother and Papucho. *Chorando se foi.* My mother and Orozco. Papucho and Flor. Muñeca and Ponciano. Muñeca and Ramoncito. Muñeca and Eduardo. Luisito and his boyfriend. *Se fue*. Esbieta and Pavel. *Sin decir adiós*. Esbieta and the old Spaniard. Alex and I... *Cuchi-cuchi*. Men and women, boys and girls, proper and mismatched couples, a hieroglyphic of tangled limbs and dangerous smells that I tried in vain to decipher. Sex.

Chapter 5

Weddings, *las bodas*...The name conjured up visions of satin dresses, white flowers, Wagner's wedding march and monumental cakes. But the "special period" had changed that too, scaling down the celebrations.

Newlyweds were allowed to buy just one meringue cake for their party. They had the right to a ceremony at *El Palacio de los Matrimonios*, the Wedding Palace where a notary public married couples in fifteen-minute intervals and a photographer took quick snapshots that didn't always come out right. Sometimes the bride's eyes looked purple and the groom's hair had a green hue.

But Esbieta was marrying a rich Spaniard and things worked differently for them. The legal ceremony would take place at *La Maison*, the fashionable Miramar boutique that also served as a wedding parlor for foreigners. Pepe planned to invite his friends and the bride's immediate family to a reception in the *La Maison* gardens. (The buffet cost thirty dollars per guest so attendance was limited, Sonia explained, embarrassed.) Later that evening they would throw a more inclusive party at the apartment. To that, I was invited.

The three hundred dollars that Pepe gave to his fiancée for her trousseau vanished as quickly as ice cream in my mouth, drier than stale bread during that summer of 1994. Sonia and I went to the "shoppings" and bought cans of Spam to make sandwiches for the party, packages of Kool-aid, jars of mayonnaise, plastic dishes, a mixer, toilet paper, and a new curtain for their bathroom.

My friend had the delicacy of not bragging about her good fortune. She was generous, too, and often invited me to a snack in El Rápido, a dollar-zone cafeteria that sold hot dogs, French fries and fruit juices. Once she even urged me to get a dress. They were on sale for seven dollars in Yumurí.

"I can't take your sister's money without her permission!" I protested, though one outfit had already caught my eye. It was blue, long and ruffled. Sort of old fashioned, but cute.

"Come on, Esbieta won't mind it. She likes you. Buy it if you want. Or get something else."

For the first time I dared to look at the merchandise as a prospective customer. Chinese sandals, Mexican soaps, Canadian coats and Cuban bonbons winked at me from the store shelves.

"*Anda*, Longina!"

I spotted another dress. It was red, shorter, sexier... I wouldn't ask for both but couldn't decide for one either.

"Which one do you like best?" I asked Sonia, feeling like Meryl Streep in *Sophie's Choice*.

"The red one."

When we left the store with our "Easy Shopping" bags, I already knew I had made a mistake. The red dress was too revealing and Ma mère wouldn't let me wear it.

But I didn't return to exchange it. Trips to dollar-zone places left me in a painful state of mind: a mix of confusion, resentment and bitterness. Why couldn't Ma mère and Orozco afford to buy in the "shoppings," though they both had university degrees and worked hard? Was it worthwhile to continue studying, to go to college? Should I leave *La Lenin* and become a *jinetera* instead? I envied Esbieta but also pitied her. How would it feel to kiss an old fat guy like Pepe? Fu!

I swore not to return with Sonia to the "shoppings."

But I couldn't refuse to accompany her to the Comodoro Hotel, where Pepe was staying. She didn't want to visit him alone.

"Sorry to ask *El Abuelo* for more money," she said, not looking sorry at all. "But we can't miss this chance. Avelina is selling five pounds of pork for fifteen dollars. A bargain! In the 'shopping,' they cost thirty-five."

The Comodoro Hotel was in the exclusive Miramar area, so far from Centro Habana that it took us two hours to get there. As we approached the lobby, the security guards stopped us. "Are you Cubans? You can't come in."

When Sonia explained that we were looking for Señor José Martínez, they eyed us suspiciously and asked "what our relationship with that comrade—er—gentleman, was."

"He's my brother-in-law," Sonia answered in a dignified tone.

The guards chortled and ogled her. "And how old is your *hermanita*?"

The receptionist finally phoned "Señor Martínez." Up close, *El Abuelo* didn't look so ugly. He had blue eyes and a neatly trimmed white beard. But my first thought was that he should be marrying Muñeca, not Esbieta.

"*Hola, chicas*," he greeted us with a thick Spanish accent.

"We need cash, *tío*," Sonia said, quite bossily.

"How much?"

"A Franklin."

He opened his wallet and handed her a hundred dollar bill. I had never seen so much money before.

"Where is Esbieta?" he asked.

"So sick that she can't get out of bed," Sonia answered. "The *pobrecita* is coming down with something, I'm afraid."

"Let me know if she needs to see a doctor," Pepe seemed sincerely concerned. "I'll take her to *Cira García.*"

Cira Garcia was a dollar-zone hospital where Pepe bought the PPG pills he used to regulate his cholesterol level, according to Esbieta. But Sonia told me that they served another purpose: *cuchi-cuchi* helpers for older men.

"Esbieta is at Guanabo beach," she said after we left the Comodoro grounds. "I didn't want to bother her now because she went with Pavel. He is young, handsome... and doesn't need to use PPG! Poor *Abuelo*. You know, I feel sorry for him. He isn't a bad guy."

"But how will Esbieta feel when she has to live with that geezer forever?"

"She'll get used to it. One gets used to everything, *Mamá* says."

That was true. Hadn't we gotten used to the "special period," the scarcity, the *cerelac*?

"What about Pavel?"

Sonia shrugged and began to sing a popular Los Van Van song, "*Nadie quiere a nadie. Se acabó el querer.*"

No one loves anybody. Love is gone.

§ § §

Classes were over. Ma mère and Orozco, pleased with my good grades and "positive" attitude toward *La Lenin*, made the summer vacation as enjoyable as possible. She bought me a pair of Lee bluejeans on the black market. He installed an electric fan in my room. Muñeca, as usual, pampered me as if I were still *la niña*, her little girl.

In that climate of family harmony I condescended to

notice my stepbrothers, Humbertico and Camilo. (The youngest had been named after Camilo Cienfuegos, a rebel commander in the Sierra Maestra Mountains.) I found out that they weren't as nosey and impertinent as I had thought. They called me their big sister and looked up to me in a flattering way. Humbertico, the oldest, would join me at *La Lenin* the following year. His father wanted him to study medicine but he wouldn't hear of it.

"The old man is out of his mind!" he said. "I'd like to be a hotel manager, a panataxi driver or a tourist guide... whatever pays enough dollars to buy a car and gas, or at least a motorcycle. I don't want to end up riding a bicycle like him."

Camilo dreamed of being a guitarist and incessantly played "Let it Be," "Hey Jude" and other Beatles songs with more determination than skill.

On the warm, humid evenings Alex and I sat on the Malecón seawall and kissed. We had become more dexterous. Elbows and noses were no longer obstacles. My family wasn't, either.

Ma mère was having a difficult pregnancy, complicated with anemia, and didn't ask where I went on Saturday nights. It made me think, at times, that she didn't care what I did anymore. She only loved Orozco and his offspring. If she was like that now, once the baby were born she wouldn't even remember my name!

"Of course she cares for you," Alex reassured me. "She's your mom. But you are a grown-up now, so she doesn't want to interfere too much."

Interfere *ni un carajo*! My boyfriend was an only child. What did he know about the dangers posed by half-siblings? His parents had been married for twenty years. I couldn't help but feel jealous. *Bueno*, at least he had seen good examples at home. We swore to stay together, forever and ever. With "this" or without "this." And we intended to keep our promise, contrary to some people I knew...

"You are my only love, *Naricitas*," he said often. "Nobody is going to separate us." Alex called me *Naricitas* because I was always complaining about the unbecoming size of my nose.

I had told Muñeca of our relationship, but only after she pledged to keep the secret. Hadn't Ma mère waited until her belly looked as big as a watermelon to shyly let me know about her pregnancy? I would tell her about Alex when I felt like it. Ah!

My boyfriend longed to be a businessman like his paternal grandfather. The old man had owned La Sortija, a well-known jewelry store, before the revolution. "I don't want to be a diplomat," he told me. "They need to wear two faces in public and a third one at home."

His parents had been *comecandelas* at first, donating the store to the government before it was nationalized. But now they were disillusioned with "this."

"They say that You-know-who takes one step forward and three backwards," Alex confided. "But when he dies, Cuba will be a prosperous country again. I'll have my own store, without coupons or ration cards. You can help me sell, or write ads for the business."

Advertisement was another new, "special period" term. A United Colors of Benetton ad had replaced the Cuban flag on the Capri Hotel façade.

Chapter 6

Plastic Christmas trees were sold, for the first time since the beginning of "this," at the dollar-zone stores. Ma mère bought a small one and placed it on our living room coffee table. Muñeca found an old silver ornament to crown it. "That's the star of Bethlehem, *la estrella de Belén*," she told me. "Now we need the Magi."

She had concluded that only the Three Kings could solve our problems. After so many post-perestroika years my grandma got disheartened and believed that, unless a miracle happened, we'd be irremediably stuck with "this." Luisito, now a subdued ticket seller at the García Lorca Theater, was of the same opinion.

I didn't contradict them because I had been sworn to secrecy. But I had hopes, and they didn't rely on the Wise Men. The *Movimiento Cristiano de Liberación*, founded in 1988 by Oswaldo Payá Sardiñas, was part of a growing national opposition network. Though the *Movimiento* was illegal, Payá already had several hundred followers. Lisaveta and her father were among them.

There were also isolated protests. During blackouts people banged pots and pans and wrote anti-government messages in public places. Colorful *gusano* graffiti covered the fading revolutionary murals. But dissidents acted at their own risk. Avelina's son went to jail after he was caught writing *Abajo Fidel* on a grocery store wall. Ten intellectuals had signed a letter in 1991, *la Carta de los Diez*, asking the government to free all prisoners of conscience. But You-know-who's response was throwing *them* in jail, too.

Payá was collecting signatures for a petition to the

Popular Power Assembly. It demanded a plebiscite like the one that had defeated Pinochet in Chile in 1989. The petitioners had to give their names, addresses and ID card numbers. At first I was convinced that nobody would sign it. If people went to jail for writing "Down with Fidel" on a wall, what would happen to those who dared to ask You-know-who to step down? That was playing with the monkey at its worst! But Lisaveta's father managed to get ninety signatures in just three weeks.

"Isn't he afraid of losing his job at *Prensa Latina*?" I asked her.

"The Berlin Wall fell when Germans learned not to be afraid," she replied. "Yes, he may be fired, even jailed. But someone has to risk his *pellejo*, his precious skin, so we all don't end up scalped."

Lisaveta's tomboyish figure suddenly took epic proportions. If more Cubans were like her, *comecandelas* wouldn't rule over the neighborhoods. We wouldn't need an exit visa to travel abroad. Papucho wouldn't have left. Voluntary work wouldn't be compulsory...

"Payá and my father aren't alone," she added. "*I* am helping, too. Would you lend us a hand?"

After a brief hesitation I agreed, feeling courageous, patriotic and half crazy. What was I getting into? But I couldn't let my friend down after she had trusted me. And the perestroika bug had bitten me too.

Every Saturday afternoon I went to the Miralles's home in El Vedado and we shut ourselves in Lisaveta's bedroom. Using two old Underwood typewriters, we copied the petition hundreds of times.

"It's a pity that we can't sign it because we're still minors," she said.

I didn't tell her that I wouldn't have had the guts to do it. She would have considered me a *pendeja*, a coward. But she was a daughter of perestroika and I, a "special period" girl.

Pedro Miralles wasn't too happy with his daughter's dissident fervor, though he didn't prohibit her from helping the *Movimiento*. But he asked us not to mention our activities to anyone else, not even boyfriends or family members. "This is serious stuff, girls. I mean, you could be expelled from *La Lenin* and sent to a juvenile detention camp." I promised to be discreet and so did Lisaveta, reluctantly.

I had a secret crush on Miralles. He was tall, with broad shoulders and a booming voice. Like Papucho, he had perfect white teeth. My puppy love was aided and abetted by the fact that he talked to me with deference and advised Lisaveta to learn from "proper, well-behaved Longina" to keep her big mouth shut. I fantasized that, if I Alex ever dumped me, I would marry Miralles. Older guys liked young *chicas*, as the amount and variety of Esbieta's partners proved. Miralles could fall in love with me—supposing I flirted with him...

Oh, had Lisaveta known of such dreams she'd have said *Qué descarada*, what a shameless girl! But it didn't look like Alex had any intention of dumping me. I was too shy to flirt. And there was Lisaveta's mother, a tough *guajira* who would have probably kicked my now round, well developed *culón*.

§ § §

Esbieta's wedding was scheduled for July 14th. "Bring anyone you want to the party," Sonia told me, "except that camouflaged *comecandela*, *la* Lisaveta. I can't stand her."

Alex wished we could go together like other couples who attended *quinceañeras* and Saturday night parties. He also wanted to meet my mother and grandma and tell them that "his intentions were serious." But despite Ma mère's recent apathy, I was concerned. What if she disliked him and began to preach, or worse, to interfere? I looked for ways to dissuade my boyfriend without hurting his feelings.

Then his father was sent to Beijing on a diplomatic mission and decided, at the last minute, to take the whole family along. Though Alex preferred to stay, his parents insisted that he accompany them. They would fly just one day before the wedding. My boyfriend was inconsolable when he gave me the news.

"But you guys will be there for only a week," I said, rubbing my nose against his. "It'll be okay."

I was secretly relieved. Besides, I planned to devote as much time as possible to Payá's project while my boyfriend was gone.

"The problem is, we are going to stop at Gander airport, in Canada," he said, looking nervous.

"*Chico*, what did you expect?" I asked, stupidly. "The plane can't get from here to Beijing without stopping somewhere, no?"

He didn't answer.

"I love you, *Naricitas*," he whispered at last. Then he kissed me and said, "*Dasvidanya*."

Dasvidanya means goodbye in Russian. But I didn't know that.

§ § §

I gave up on going to the beach that year. The Cárdenas girls were spending the summer in Madrid after their father got a job at a Cuban-Spanish joint venture. Orozco didn't have gasoline for a trip to Guanabo, much less to

Varadero, and "camels" passed every three hours. The city didn't offer much entertainment either. Waiting lines in the Coppelia's peso area (part of it was dollar-only now) reached the Yara Movie Theater, across the street, where the same old movies were shown for several weeks. There was nothing to do, nowhere to go. Only Esbieta's wedding day glowed in the grayness of the summer vacation like the star of Bethlehem.

My first grown-up party! Even without Alex, I couldn't wait to go. But, as if Ponciano's spirit had put a curse on it, things turned out badly right from the start. First, I lost my bangs trying to turn them into ringlets. Muñeca's curling iron was responsible for the failure. My hair began spouting smoke and I was left with a bunch of singed locks. To describe the results, I resorted to a vulgar expression that had become popular: my hair sucked. "*Está de culo*," I said.

"Don't say *groserías*, Longina," Ma mère scolded me.

Then I tried on the red dress that Sonia had chosen for me at Yumurí.

"People are going to think that you are a *jinetera*, *niña*," my grandma said. "Wear something else."

"Look who's talking," I grumbled. Even Muñeca sucked. I ended up wearing a pair of jeans and a Pan-American Games T-shirt.

During the ceremony at *La Maison* I waited in Sonia's apartment. There were so many guests that I couldn't find a place to sit.

"Have your rice ready when *los novios* come in," Avelina told me. "It brings good luck to throw it over newlyweds."

That practice had almost disappeared because of the rationing, but Sonia's mother bought enough rice at the "shopping" to give each of us a small cup. I saw a neighbor hide her portion in a ragged vinyl purse.

Young women with big butts, long nails and short miniskirts filled the apartment with the fragrance of foreign perfumes. Slick guys in Jordache jeans and sleeveless shirts, with huge gold chains around their necks, escorted them. I recognized Pavel, a tall, handsome mulatto with sad eyes. What was he doing there?

Esbieta and Pepe returned from *La Maison* in a red, remodeled, chrome-happy '53 Cadillac. Sonia, Mónica and their mother followed in a touristaxi and there was a third car, a black Mercedes-Benz where the groom's friends had piled in.

"*Vivan los novios*!" Avelina yelled.

A rain of rice covered the mismatched couple as they entered the living room. Esbieta's dress was a dream of frills and white lace. Her sequined satchel sparkled. But two wrinkles that I had never seen crossed her round, pretty face, making her look tired and older.

"With all the money they are spending on this travesty I could eat for three months," the woman who had stolen the rice said. "But I don't blame Esbieta. If I were young and beautiful I'd be a *jinetera* too."

Pavel flushed and I thought he was going to insult her. But he just walked away. Esbieta's eyes followed him as he silently left the apartment. *Chorando se foi*.

The groom's friends arrived, carrying wine bottles. Sonia's mother brought half of the ornamented wedding cake that they had shared at *La Maison*. Avelina asked where the punch bowl was.

I felt an urge to leave. What was *I* doing there? My old T-shirt looked shabby, more so when compared to the other girls' elegant clothes. My hair sucked. Sonia wouldn't have time to even talk to me with so many people around...Without saying goodbye I scurried outside. Pavel was already in the street, busily scratching the surface of the red Cadillac.

§ § §

Muñeca was surprised to see me back so soon.

"I got bored," I lied. "Parties suck."

"Lisaveta called and said she wanted to see you," Ma mère told me.

"I'm going to her house, then," I said. "*Chao.*"

"Why don't you wait until tomorrow? It's dangerous to go out alone this late."

"It's only nine o'clock. I'll be back before midnight. Besides, would you care if something happened to me?" I asked, glancing at her inflated belly.

"Longina!" Ma mère jumped up. "What do you mean? Of course I would care! Why do you ask such a question? You are my daughter!"

"But soon I won't be the only one," I replied. "And you—you change your mind about everything. You forgot Papucho in a heartbeat. Now you're a *comecandela.*"

"*Niña...*"

She tried to hug me, but I backed off. And I couldn't shut up. "You are going to have another baby. *Orejón*'s baby. How do I know that you still love me? You only like him now!"

"You are too young to understand. . . "

"I am not *that* young. I do understand a few things now. You are so. . . ," I fought to find the right word, "Unstable."

She lowered her eyes. "Is it about politics?"

"Yes. Well, yes and no. It's about everything."

"I did love Papucho. And I'm as sad as you are about his—departure. But I couldn't live with him anymore. He was a drunk, you know it. He wasn't going to sober up."

"But..."

She made me sit next to her. "I do try to agree with Humberto, to reconcile our views. *La revolución* is important to him. And if family peace depends on me going to a Red Sunday or voluntary work, I'll go. Living together is difficult, Longina, and something has to give. But you are my daughter, *mi niña*. That will never change, hear?"

I nodded, but wasn't yet convinced.

"I won't love you less because of the new baby," she went on. "And in a few years you will have other interests. You'll go to college, marry, maybe have your own kids... And then you'll really understand the give and take of life, the delicate balance that keeps a *núcleo familiar* together."

"When I get married, I'll make sure that we both think the same of 'this,'" I whispered. But I still hugged her before leaving for Lisaveta's house.

I walked to El Vedado after waiting in vain for the M-3 "camel." My friend opened the door with such a somber face that I feared the worst. "What happened?" I asked, thinking that the *Movimiento* leaders had been imprisoned and that, of course, we would be next.

"A tugboat was sunk yesterday," she said. "More than thirty people died—women and children, too. They tried to flee the country and were killed by the Cuban Coast Guard."

We sat by her father's short-wave radio and listened to the reports transmitted by Radio Martí, the Voice of America, Radio France and other foreign stations. They all agreed that the Coast Guard was following You-know-who's orders.

"The bastard!" Lisaveta repeated. "Someone has to shoot him!"

I was sad and enraged. You-know-who sucked. So did the Cuban Coast Guard. And "this." And life itself. But I didn't understand why Lisaveta had made me come all the way from Centro Habana to share that awful news. On a Saturday evening of all times!

"I'm sorry, I almost forgot why I called you," she said after a while. "Alex and his parents defected in Canada. They were sick and tired of 'this.' He asked me to tell you that he still loves you and hopes to see you again, someday."

Se fue sin decir adiós.

§ § §

"The good thing about 'this' is how bad it is getting."

After the tugboat sinking, not even the most ardent *comecandelas* dared defend "this" in public. People got angrier as details of the "accident" (as the Cuban government insisted on calling it) spread. Rage took over Havana sweeping Che Guevara's posters, You-know-who's billboards, murals with revolutionary slogans and Benetton ads. No one whispered anymore. They yelled and wrote *gusano* messages in broad daylight. At bus stops, inside crowded "camels" and in the endless waiting lines they cursed You-know-who and called him a murderer.

Despite his love for "*la revolución*" Orozco agreed that the government had gone too far this time. "The tugboat passengers didn't have a chance," he said, "And there were kids aboard. How could they do it?"

The answer was simple: *Se acabó el querer.* Love was gone.

Papucho could have suffered the same fate. How many rafts and boats had been sunk before? How many times had the Cuban Coast Guard killed clandestine rafters? Yes, love was gone.

Love was also Alex and his promises of always being together. His family had settled in Saskatoon, Lisaveta told me. I needed to look at a Canadian map to find out where the city was, up there in *casa del carajo.* The ballad *Muñe*ca used to sing in San Anastasio Street came back like a fulfilled prophecy.

Se fue para no volver,
Se fue sin decirme adiós.
Muy lejos de mí se fue
Matando mi ensueño de amor. . .

To which I added a new verse, a salsa rhythm propelled by wild drums,

Se acabó el querer.

My poor Muñeca was drifting away. She spent hours talking about (and sometimes to) her past loves. She sat in a rocking chair to sing *Se fue* and sometimes cried. She didn't cry for any man in particular but for her own lost youth. For the beauty and *sandunga* that had also left her, never to return. She recalled incessantly the good times she had had at the Colony House and regretted not having stayed in Miami with a handsome, wealthy young man named Felo. She asked Ponciano's spirit if he still loved her.

Se acabó el querer.

Ma mère waited for the birth of her child with more anxiety than joy. She had just been laid off. Gente Nueva didn't have enough paper to publish new books and editors were sent home "until things improved," they were told. But rumor had it that the *Palacio del Segundo Cabo* would be transformed into a dollar-zone hotel, like most of La Habana Vieja historic buildings.

Other people had also lost their jobs. Luisito was fired from the García Lorca Theater because the manager found out that he had a boyfriend. "Other guys have partners for years and they are never caught," he complained. "Antonio and I have been together only for three months and paf! The cat is out of the bag. But that was just an excuse to get rid of me. Why should they care about a ticket seller's private life? It's not as if I had been a ballet star."

Sonia's mother was working only half time because there were no spare parts to fix the made-in-the-USSR sewing machines. Our neighbor Mauricio had returned to Chile, disillusioned with the regime he had once wished to see established in his country. Life looked grim.

For the first time my family couldn't make ends meet. The four of us lived on Orozco's salary, the equivalent of fifteen dollars a month. And he was still paying child support. We couldn't afford black market prices anymore.

Instead of *café con leche* I drank a glass of water with brown sugar every night. Ma mère learned to fry eggs in water. It was healthier than using oil, Nitza Villapol stated on *Cocina al Minuto*. Following her advice we began to eat the potato skins "because all the nutrients were concentrated there."

Muñeca, who couldn't digest the *cerelac*, looked "underdeveloped." Her once colossal behind melted down. Ma mère resembled a snake that had swallowed a rock. Orozco started growing a beard because razor blades didn't "come" to the stores anymore. After toothpaste disappeared we resorted to baking powder. When available, laundry detergent doubled as soap.

"Camels" passed every three or four hours. A new job was created: *los amarillos*, the yellow guys. Wearing bright yellow uniforms, they stopped every car that passed by the bus stop and asked (begged, ordered) the drivers to give people a ride. "Zero option" was just around the corner.

Or wasn't it?

Because the "shoppings" were still full of Chinese sandals, Mexican soaps, Canadian chickens and Cuban bonbons. Anybody with dollars could buy them. The number of panataxis and touristaxis had increased, along with the amount of young *jineteras* who rode in them. *Paladares*, small private restaurants, offered typical Cuban meals like pork, rice and black beans for seven or eight dollars.

Orozco still cycled to Lawton every day and came home exhausted. He wanted to find a job at a hotel or at least in a *paladar*. "I can be a doorman or a cook," he said. "Anything, as long as it pays dollars."

The former Habana Libre, now Habana-Meliá, the Meliá-Cohiba, the Capri and many hotels now belonged to Cuban-Spanish joint ventures known as *corporaciones*. They paid their employees a small percentage in dollars and gave them a bag with cooking oil, soap and spaghetti every month. *Mayimbes* like General Cárdenas controlled the Cuban side of the business. Putting his pride in his pocket, Orozco went to see a former Army colonel who had fought in the Sierra Maestra Mountains with him and was a Meliá-Cohiba hotel manager.

"There are fifteen candidates for every job opening here," the *mayimbe* told him. "The Spaniards want young, good-looking, English-speaking people. I'm sorry, comrade."

My stepfather returned home crestfallen. He didn't have better luck with the *paladares*' owners.

After two months of entreaties, calls and humiliations, he finally got a job cooking hamburgers and hot dogs at Burguis, a dollar-only cafeteria on Infanta Street. He began to "resolve" meat, bread and butter. All his coworkers did the same, so he didn't worry about being accused of diversion of resources. The members of our *núcleo familiar* began to gain weight again. But exchanging his immaculate medical gown for a greasy T-shirt had a demoralizing effect on Orozco, who had prided himself for years on being "the doctor."

"I never dreamed I would end up waiting tables for food," he complained. "After all I have done for 'this!'"

Ay, naïve, selfless, hardworking Boxer...Orozco should have read *Animal Farm*, no matter how ideologically deviant he thought the book was.

He didn't listen to You-know-who's speeches anymore. On the 26th of July, he refused to turn on the TV and spent the evening reading Ma mère's old copies of the *Reader's Digest*. His love affair with *la revolución* was over.

Se acabó el querer.

Despite their *international relations*, things weren't rosy for Sonia's family either. Her brother got caught selling Cohiba cigars to a Colombian near the Capri Hotel and was sentenced to two years in jail for harassing a tourist.

Old Pepe, in Barcelona, tried to expedite Esbieta's trip. Besides the Cuban exit permit, she needed the *Libro de Familia*, a document issued by the Spanish embassy. The process to get it took months because thousands of children, grandchildren and even great-grandchildren of Spanish immigrants were now claiming their ancestors' citizenship in order to leave Cuba. Waiting lines in front of the embassy were five blocks long.

Pavel had broken up with Esbieta after the wedding. She was depressed and cried every day.

"She wants to dump Pepe but that would be a very stupid thing to do now," Sonia said. "Even *Mamá* tells her that she's already riding the donkey. She has to finish the race."

"But she still loves Pavel," I reminded her.

"Are we going to eat love?"

Se acabó el querer.

"This" had to change. But how? Who would dare to challenge You-know-who? After Ochoa's execution and the tugboat sinking, where was the hero willing to risk his beloved *pellejo* for his fellow citizens' sake?

Zero option loomed on the horizon: a primitive community where people ate potatoes (skin included), lived in tents, farmed with oxen and sang *La Internacional* under the light of an unreachable star of Bethlehem.

Chapter 7

It was the fifth of August when Lisaveta called and said that her father had received a letter for me.

"It's an email from Alex," she explained. "You'll have to go to *Prensa Latina* and read it there because the printer doesn't work."

I didn't have the faintest idea of what an email was, but hurried to the *Prensa Latina* offices. Miralles let me sit at his computer and showed me how to use it. Was that science fiction or what? Alex had sent the message the night before, from Saskatoon, and it was already in Havana! My heart pounding, I read the words that seemed to have traveled at the speed of light through space and time.

Querida Longina,

I haven't forgotten you, *Naricitas*. I think of you every day. Wait for me. Things are going to change soon and then either I will return to Havana or send for you.

You would like it here. On weekends I walk by the Saskatchewan River and see squirrels and chipmunks. People are friendly and ask lots of questions about Cuba and You-know-who. Some ask funny things like what language we speak there and if everybody smokes big cigars.

Dad is working in a cannery. *Mamushka* hasn't found a job yet. They want me to start high school in September but my English is poor. I don't think I can make it.

It's warm now. But in the winter one can shoot an elk and leave it outside for three months, a neighbor told me. It won't spoil because the temperature drops to twenty degrees below zero. I hope that before winter comes we can go back to Cuba, or at least move to Miami.

I'm at a cybercafé and used all my Internet credit, so I have to stop here. I miss you. Write to me.

Hugs, many hugs and kisses on your cute little nose,

Alex

Miralles told me that I could write back to my boyfriend if I brought the letter ready and didn't take more than ten minutes to type it. I was so happy that I jumped and kissed him. *Qué descarada*!

On my way home I smiled to everybody and didn't understand why passersby looked at me funny.

Love wasn't gone, after all.

I stopped by Sonia's apartment to share the good news with her. She had some news of her own. Her brother had been freed after they gave three hundred dollars to a captain of the *Policía Nacional Revolucionaria*. And the day before, thanks to Pepe's connections in Spain, Esbieta had gotten the *Libro de Familia.*

"Well, congratulations!" I said. "This is a beautiful world, isn't it?"

"Not really, *chica*," Esbieta replied. "It sucks."

Later Sonia told me that her sister had bought fifty diazepam pills on the black market. Their mother was afraid that she would take them all at once.

"Maybe she should stay here with Pavel," Sonia said thoughtfully. "But even Esbieta doesn't want her children to grow up in a *barbacoa* as we did. And they have no other place to go. It's not easy, my friend."

That was another "special period" phrase. It's not easy. *No es fácil*, everybody complained.

When I got home Humbertico and Camilo asked me

if I had heard about the riots in La Habana Vieja.

"People are shattering the shop windows in the dollar zone," Camilo said. "They are shouting '*Libertad*' and 'Down with Fidel.' And plain-clothed cops are there and Special Brigade guys with clubs, and they're hitting rioters but rioters are throwing rocks at them!"

"You-know-who went and tried to talk to the protesters, but they wouldn't listen to him," Humbertico added. "They would have thrown rocks at him too, if his bodyguards hadn't been there."

Camilo started singing a Willy Chirino song, *Ya viene llegando*.

"Our day is coming," he chanted. "Our day is coming, at last!"

But was it coming, really? Would You-know-who's kingdom fall like the Berlin Wall? Could the riots mean the end of "this"?

I wanted to see for myself but Ma mère didn't allow me to leave the house. She locked all the doors and Orozco forbade his sons to go out again.

"When Machado fled in 1933, people raided the houses of the *machadistas* and dragged them down the streets," Muñeca said. "It was a bloodbath. Weren't you a *machadista*, Orozco?

"Mother, he wasn't even born in 1933," Ma mère replied, looking uncomfortable. "How could he be a *machadista*?"

"I mean, a *fidelista*. What's the difference?"

I called Lisaveta but no one answered. For all I knew, she could be throwing rocks at the police as the Timisoara students had done in Rumania.

Humbertico, Camilo and I sat in the living room—we weren't even allowed to go out to the porch—and planned our future in whispers. If "this" changed, Humbertico would consider becoming a doctor. Up to then he had wanted to be a hotel manager or a touristaxi driver. "But I heard that doctors make tons of money in capitalist countries," he said seriously, "Like five hundred dollars a month." Camilo still wanted to be a guitarist. He would travel all over the world, like Willy Chirino, when exit permits were no longer necessary. I would go to Miami and try to find Papucho, then fly to Saskatoon and meet Alex. Or my boyfriend would come back and we all would support Oswaldo Payá's presidential campaign...

All night long Ma mère and Orozco listened to the Voice of America and Radio Martí. The jamming was stronger than ever. The reporters' voices faded in and out. News stories were confusing and often contradictory.

"The Regla ferryboat was hijacked by ten desperate Cubans and taken to Florida."

"Castro threatens the Clinton administration with another Mariel boatlift."

"Forty percent of the Miami Cubans will return to the island as soon as Castro's regime falls."

Miami Cubans. Would Papucho come back?

Two days later rumors got wilder. An enraged crowd had attacked the Deauville Hotel, clashing with security guards. Several rioters had been shot, others imprisoned. There had been other attempts to hijack the Regla ferryboat. You-know-who had declared that "the Cuban Coast Guard wouldn't present obstacles to those who wanted to abandon the island." *El* Malecón was full of rafts and boats.

I tried again to call Lisaveta but her phone had been disconnected. Had she left, too? She said she never would. But hadn't I already learned not to trust anyone?

The next morning Luisito showed up. He was accompanied by another guy that I assumed was his boyfriend, Antonio. Luisito approached my grandma, who was absentmindedly sitting on her rocking chair, chanting to herself, and whispered, "I came to say goodbye to you, Muñeca."

"Where are you going, my son?"

"To *La Yuma*. It's too late to see my mother or become a ballet dancer, but at least I'll start a new life."

"Your mother...Is she still living on San Anastasio Street? Give her my regards."

"I will."

Luisito kissed my grandma's forehead and left. I reached him by the door.

"I'm sorry," I said. "Muñeca's mind is..."

"I understand, Longina."

"Are you leaving on a raft?"

"Yes, Antonio and I made one."

Antonio beamed. "It's a really good one, girl. See, we used two dining room tables, a sofa and the motor of an old Chevy."

"But the waves, the sharks...Aren't you afraid?"

"You bet we are," Luisito said. "But I already missed the Mariel boatlift. I can't afford to miss this one too. See, I'm almost forty years old. This is my last chance."

They left together, hand in hand. I wished them good luck and returned to the living room.

"He's going to meet his mama," Muñeca said. "How sweet."

I shuddered.

I wasn't still allowed to go out. During that time of forced inactivity, Ma mère found a way to keep me at home.

"Let's go through dad's papers," she proposed, scratching her swollen belly. "Maybe we'll find that poetry book you always wanted to read."

When we moved to Zapata Street all the boxes that had been in Ponciano's bedroom were placed in the garage. Nobody had the time or the interest to open them. Busy with school and friends, I had almost forgotten Doña Lola. But the old curiosity came back. I started emptying out cardboard boxes with my stepbrothers' help.

"We may find an envelope with ten thousand pesos inside," Humbertico said, encouraging.

There were old, discolored magazines (*Bohemia*, *Vanidades*, *Social*) published in the forties and fifties. *The Imitation of Christ*. Dale Carnegie's *How to Win Friends and Influence People*. (What had Ponciano learned from it?) Pages from *El Mundo*, *La Marina* and other newspapers that had disappeared long before I was born....

Camilo, who was allergic to dust, sneezed uncontrollably. But it was he who found two notebooks neatly tied with pink ribbons.

"Here you are," he told me, coughing.

The manuscript smelled of mold and vaguely of mice. My heart pounding, I untied the ribbons.

The phone rang.

"It's Sonia," Ma mère said, coming in the garage. "Oh, did you find it? Let me see."

Talk about inopportune timing! I handed her the manuscript, went back to the house and lifted the receiver, "Yes, Sonia."

"Longina, come here at once," her voice was barely audible. "It's important."

"Sorry, I can't leave now," I answered. "I'll see you in an hour or so."

"Then it will be too late. Don't waste any time. It's now or never!"

With that melodramatic phrase she hung up. I would have gladly run to Carlos III Avenue. But there was Doña Lola's manuscript, waiting for me to read it. "*Oh, mi aldea...cuánto el alma se recrea al volverte a contemplar*," I whispered, like a long overdue homage to my great-grandmother.

I felt torn. Yet I could look at the manuscript later. The dusty pages weren't going anywhere. And Sonia didn't get excited easily. What if she had something *really* important to tell me?

"Okay," I said to myself. "I'm going! *Cómo joden*!"

After much pleading, Ma mère gave me permission to go out.

"Come back soon," she said. "If you see people yelling or a police car, cross the street and don't get involved, hear?"

A small crowd had gathered in front of the building where my friends lived. Sonia, her mother, sisters and brother and even Pavel were there. The two guys struggled to lift what looked like a raft.

"Hey, Longina!" Sonia yelled. "You want to go, don't you?"

Go? Where? Before I could answer, a couple carrying a similar conveyance approached us.

"In half an hour we'll be in Malecón Drive, buddy," the man said to Pavel.

"Half an hour?" Pavel laughed. "Twenty minutes, I bet you. Come on, everybody! We have to get out of here before You-know-who blinks and changes his mind!"

I stared at the rafts, the "magnum opus" of prospective *balseros* who had never been at sea.

Esbieta, clinging to her boyfriend, looked happier and younger than on her wedding day. It didn't matter that she now wore an old ragged pair of jeans and a T-shirt nor that, instead of the sequined satchel, she carried an "Easy Shopping" plastic bag.

"What does this mean?" I asked Sonia.

"Where have you been, *chica*? You-know-who said on TV that anyone who wanted to leave could do it. He's scared, for the first time. He's afraid of the rioters. This is the only chance we have!"

In a daze I walked along with the group, joining dozens of families that carried boats and rafts, lifesavers, and bottles of water. It looked like a big, joyful public party. A woman dressed in white, a *santera*, held a life-size image of the Virgin of Regla.

Once we reached Malecón Drive, the *balseros* threw their rafts into the ocean. Questions, warnings, jubilant cries and goodbyes billowed like farewell banners in the Caribbean breeze.

"Love you, *mamá*!"

"Be careful of the sharks."

"Do you have enough water?

"See you in Miami."

"*Adiós*."

And those who were already aboard the rafts lifted their arms and chanted, *A remar, a remar, a remar. Que la virgen de Regla nos va a acompañar*. Let's row, let's row, let's row, the virgin of Regla will accompany us...

Esbieta hugged her mother while her brother and Pavel dragged the raft across the rocky Malecón shore.

"Are you sure you don't want to come, *Mamá*?" Esbieta asked.

Her mother pointed to little Mónica, who watched the scene with startled eyes.

"You, Sonia and your brother are old enough to make decisions for yourselves," she said. "But I can't risk this girl's life. If something happened..." and she crossed herself. "I just can't."

"*Ay, Mamá*! What can be worse than what we have already gone through? The 'special period,' the blackouts, the informers, the *barbacoa*, old Pepe, the *Libro de Familia*... Speaking of which," Esbieta opened her bag and threw a stack of papers to the waves, "Goodbye, *Abuelo*! Goodbye, Barcelona! Miami, here we come!"

She ran toward the shore to help Pavel. Svelte, long-haired and with a smile of triumph in her round face, she looked like the Virgin of Regla herself. And watching that dark-skinned, sinewy, handsome Pavel, I could easily understand why the *Libro de Familia* pages were now floating away.

"I called you because I want you to come with us," Sonia said to me. "May she, Pavel?"

"Sure."

"Well, I...," her offer took me by surprise. "What am I going to do in Miami?"

I didn't know if Cecilia was still alive, or if *Tío* Armando and *Tía* Jacinta, the former *comecandelas*, would welcome me.

"What everybody does, *chica*—live!"

The raft was finally on the water, buffeted by waves much taller than the hopeful *balseros* who were soon to dare them.

Someone called my name. I looked around and there was Lisaveta, sweaty and panting.

"You aren't leaving, are you?" she asked me, point-blank.

"Yes, she is," Sonia said.

Lisaveta glared at Sonia who stuck her tongue at her. They looked like silly characters in a Soviet cartoon.

"Let's go," Sonia pushed me. "Pavel's waiting for us."

Every time I eyed the raft it seemed smaller, more fragile. A dot in the blue immensity. A shark's snack.

"Please, Longina, stay," Lisaveta said. "Who will bring perestroika to Cuba if everybody leaves? *La Yuma*'s road is not the temple's road."

"Temple's road *ni un carajo*!" Sonia replied. "I always knew that you were a *comecandela*. Stay here and kiss You-know-who's beard if you wish, but leave others alone."

"I am not a *comecandela*. My father lost his job because he was fighting them. I won't be allowed to go back to *La Lenin* this fall. But I'm staying anyway."

"What happened to Miralles?" I asked.

"An informer found out that he was working with Payá. *Prensa Latina* fired him."

The three of us stayed silent.

"I'm taking something with me," Sonia said quietly. She showed Lisaveta the Cuban flag pin she had been given when we were chasing Pan-American Games visitors. "*Mira*."

"Come on, girls!" Pavel yelled.

Only a few months before, I had needed to choose between the red and the blue dresses. I had let Sonia do it and the results—sucked. This time around, no one else would decide for me.

Two paths for my future lay ahead. The bearded sovereign that at first I had called Fidel, then *El Comandante* and finally You-know-who, presided over the Cuban side. Papucho might be on the foreign side, that distant, almost mythical land known as *La Yuma*. Between them was the Caribbean: tall waves, sharks and the possibility of ending up at the bottom, a citizen forever of the Virgin of Regla's kingdom.

But the Cuban side was also Ma mère, Muñeca, even *Orejón* and my stepbrothers. The mausoleum in the Havana cemetery. And Doña Lola's manuscript.

"*Oh, mi aldea...cuánto el alma se recrea al volverte a contemplar.*"

"You are staying," Sonia said, shaking her head. It wasn't really a question but I nodded. She hugged me and, after a brief hesitation, did the same with Lisaveta, "If you ever bring perestroika here, I'll come back," she told her.

Sonia's mother, Mónica, Lisaveta and I stood together. Amid the eager rafters that jumped into the sea we stood. The rafts moved toward the horizon while the *balseros*' song floated above the waves,

A remar, a remar, a remar. Que la virgen de Regla nos va a acompañar.

CPSIA information can be obtained at www.ICGtesting.com
Printed in the USA
LVOW081713101011
249885LV00003B/135/P

9 781888 205374